CW00543522

WITTGENSTEIN'S T
LOGICO-PHILOSC

Continuum Reader's Guides

WITTGENSTEIN'S *TRACTATUS LOGICO-PHILOSOPHICUS*

Reader's Guide

ROGER M. WHITE

continuum

Continuum International Publishing Group
The Tower Building
11 York Road
London SE1 7NX

80 Maiden Lane,
Suite 704
New York, NY 10038

© Roger M. White 2006

All rights reserved. No part of this publication may be reproduced or
transmitted in any form or by any means, electronic or mechanical,
including photocopying, recording, or any information storage or retrieval
system, without prior permission in writing from the publishers.

Roger M. White has asserted his right under the Copyright, Designs and
Patents Act, 1988, to be identified as Author of this work

British Library Cataloguing-in-Publication Data
A catalogue record for this book is available from the British Library.

ISBN: 0826486177 (hardback) 0826486185 (paperback)

Library of Congress Cataloging-in-Publication Data
A catalog record for this book is available from the Library of Congress.

Typeset by Servis Filmsetting Ltd, Manchester
Printed and bound in Great Britain by
Cromwell Press Ltd, Trowbridge, Wiltshire

CONTENTS

PREFACE

As its title implies, this book is intended as a guide for people who are engaged in the study of Wittgenstein's *Tractatus*. What this means is that although it is written in such a way that it *can* be read without simultaneously reading the *Tractatus* itself, it is intended to be read by a reader who is studying the main text in such a way that they can refer to the guide while reading the *Tractatus* and *vice versa*.

The *Tractatus* is a difficult text, and as a result there is considerable controversy as to its correct interpretation, not only in the detailed exegesis of particular paragraphs, but even over the question of what the book is about. There is no book on the *Tractatus* which will not provoke disagreement at some point or other. Inevitably I have developed in this guide a particular narrative, giving my own picture of the structure of the *Tractatus* and my interpretation of the key paragraphs, while indicating at various points where alternative readings have been offered. In the light of this, the reader should never simply accept what any author says when they write about the *Tractatus*, but always check what is said against the actual text. This obviously applies to the present guide as much as to any other work on the *Tractatus*.

Less obviously, this also applies to what Wittgenstein himself writes about the *Tractatus* in the *Philosophical Investigations*. Many readers will approach the *Tractatus* after having first encountered his later philosophy. One of the points of controversy in the current debate about the *Tractatus* is the extent of the continuity in Wittgenstein's philosophy from the early to the late period of his thinking. My own view is that both the continuities and the discontinuities have been underestimated. The continuities have been underestimated in that he is for much of the time addressing precisely the same fundamental issues in the *Investigations* as he had been addressing earlier, and his later work can only be properly understood if it is seen in relation to the problems of the *Tractatus*. The discontinuities have been underestimated in that he *radically* rejects the approach he had earlier adopted to those problems. It does not go without saying that his later thoughts are always better than his first thoughts. My own view is that many of the best insights of the *Tractatus* are in danger of being lost if you assume that the *Investigations* always supersedes Wittgenstein's earlier work. In any case, the reader should first judge the *Tractatus* on its own terms, and only then try to assess what Wittgenstein says about it later. The *Tractatus* should first be interpreted in its proper context – the debate initiated by Frege and continued by Russell. Whereas the *Tractatus* belonged to the context within which the *Investigations* was written, the *Investigations* was no part of the context of the *Tractatus*.

The other point to stress about the *Tractatus* is that it is frequently assumed that Wittgenstein was a purely intuitive thinker who presented his main positions without argument. The opposite seems to me to be the case. What is true is that his arguments are indicated rather than spelled out. In the present guide I have paid particular attention to teasing out not just what Wittgenstein was saying, but also the underlying arguments that lay behind the aphoristic presentation of his case.

I should like to thank various people both for discussions about the *Tractatus* and for assistance in the preparation of this book. I am grateful to Stig Hansen, Jonathan Hodge, Justin Ions, Eugenio Lombardo, Andrew McGonigal, Peter Simons, and, above all my wife Gabrielle, whose assistance has been invaluable throughout the writing of this book. I have also benefitted greatly from the workshops on the *Tractatus* that have been held over the last few years at Stirling University, and from discussions with Peter Sullivan in particular. Finally, I have appreciated the unfailing helpfulness of the editors of this series during the preparation of this book.

CHAPTER 1

CONTEXT

WITTGENSTEIN'S LIFE UP TO THE PUBLICATION OF THE *TRACTATUS*

Ludwig Josef Johann Wittgenstein was born in Vienna in 1889. He was the youngest of eight children in the family of Karl and Leopoldine Wittgenstein. His father, Karl, was a wealthy iron and steel magnate, who also made his home a centre of musical life in Vienna, with, for example, Brahms as a frequent visitor. Karl arranged for Brahms' benefit a private performance of the Brahms Clarinet Quintet at the Wittgenstein home.

Ludwig went to study engineering in Berlin, going on to research in aeronautical engineering at Manchester. While there he became interested in the foundations of mathematics, possibly after reading Bertrand Russell's *Principles of Mathematics*, a work that impressed him deeply. This determined him to study the foundations of mathematics and, according to what looks the most reliable account, he went to ask Gottlob Frege how he should pursue his studies further. Frege advised him to go to Cambridge to work under Russell. In 1911 Wittgenstein moved to Cambridge, and worked with Russell for five terms beginning the logical enquiries that would eventually become the *Tractatus Logico-Philosophicus*, the subject of this present book. In 1912, he moved to Norway to continue work in solitude. Then came the First World War. Wittgenstein enlisted in the Austrian Army, continuing his logical work while on active service. The *Tractatus* was completed towards the end of the war when he was on leave staying with his uncle. He returned to the front, and was taken into captivity having with him a manuscript of the *Tractatus*.

Copies of the manuscript were sent to Frege and Russell. To Wittgenstein's bitter disappointment, Frege reacted unfavourably, mainly objecting to the way that the book had been set out; his correspondence with Wittgenstein suggests he had scanty understanding of the work. It looks as if he had been so put off by the layout that he had made little attempt to penetrate the content of the book. Russell, however, was impressed and wrote the Introduction that now accompanies the work. Wittgenstein, however, reacted violently to this Introduction:

> When I got the German translation of the introduction, I couldn't bring myself to have it printed with my work after all. For the fineness of your English style was – of course – quite lost and what was left was superficiality and misunderstanding.[1]

(Although Wittgenstein's reaction is understandable since Russell has misrepresented or failed to grasp some of the points that were particularly important to Wittgenstein, there is also much in the Introduction that is helpful.) Since the inclusion of Russell's Introduction was a condition of the work's publication, Wittgenstein eventually swallowed his pride, and the *Tractatus* was published by Routledge and Kegan Paul in 1922, with a translation, officially by C.K. Ogden, but with the major part of the work on the translation being undertaken by Frank Ramsey.

INTELLECTUAL INFLUENCES ON WITTGENSTEIN

In a note he made in 1931, Wittgenstein gives a list of those who had influenced his thinking. The list runs: 'Boltzmann, Hertz, Schopenhauer, Frege, Russell, Kraus, Loos, Weininger, Spengler, Sraffa'. Before going on to give a sketch of the ideas of Frege and Russell, the two thinkers who most deeply influenced Wittgenstein when he was writing the *Tractatus*, it is worth commenting on a few of the other names mentioned here.

Wittgenstein had a youthful enthusiasm for Schopenhauer as an adolescent, and apart from Frege and Russell he is the only philosopher on this list. Under Schopenhauer's influence, Wittgenstein had embraced a form of idealist philosophy during his adolescence. The ghost of Schopenhauer can be detected at some points in the *Tractatus*, but by then for the most part only as a ghost to be exorcized.

Earlier, Wittgenstein had wanted to study under Ludwig Boltzmann. Both he and Heinrich Hertz were physicists for whom

Wittgenstein expressed admiration. Their interest in scientific theories as models may have been one of the inspirations for Wittgenstein's picture theory of propositions (see 4.04).[2]

If there is an influence of Karl Kraus, it is of a very different kind. Kraus, who edited and wrote for the magazine *Die Fackel*, declared that: 'My language is the common prostitute that I turn into a virgin'. A major part of his concern was a polemical attack on the misuse of language in verbiage, inflated rhetoric and euphemism; for instance, in the First World War, he confronted the evasions of the official military communiqués with the reality of what they actually meant on the ground. I believe that it is not fanciful to see his influence behind Wittgenstein's declaring that 'the whole meaning of the *Tractatus* can be summed up roughly as follows: whatever can be said at all can be said clearly, and what we cannot speak about we must be silent about' (Preface, p. 27), or the 'demand for determinacy of sense' (3.23), where, given any proposition, we must be able to say what it amounts to in terms of the simple concrete states of affairs that constitute the world, or else reject the proposition as nonsense.

However, the major influences are Frege and Russell, whose ideas we will meet throughout this book. Here I will give a brief outline of the relevant parts of their work as a preliminary orientation for reading the *Tractatus*.

Frege

Frege's life's work was devoted to the project that came to be known as 'logicism' – a defence of the thesis that truths of arithmetic and number theory are disguised truths of logic, so that after substituting for the specifically mathematical notions such as 'number', 'addition', etc., you arrive at something that can be shown to be derivable from axioms belonging to pure logic.

We can see Frege's attempt to carry through this task as divided into three stages, corresponding to his three books: the *Begriffsschrift* (1879), *The Foundations of Arithmetic* (1884) and *The Basic Laws of Arithmetic* (vol. I, 1893 and vol. II, 1903).

The first part of the task was to develop an account of logic that was sufficiently powerful for the task. It would be absurd to suppose that the whole of arithmetic could be derived purely within the confines of Aristotelian logic. It was because Aristotle had only recognized a limited range of logical forms and there had been so little

significant advance on what he had achieved in the centuries that followed, that logic had remained an essentially sterile discipline. The
revolution in logic that Frege brought about is originally sketched
out in the *Begriffsschrift*. The crucial point to understand here is his
discovery of 'quantification theory', a radically new approach to the
problem of generality – of propositions involving the concepts of *all*,
each, *every*, *some*, etc. Aristotelian logic was built around such propositions as 'All men are mortal' and 'Some men are mortal', but was
incapable of handling more complex generalities – specifically propositions of mixed multiple generality, where the propositions contained both a sign of universal generality, such as 'every' or 'all', and
a sign of existential generality, such as 'some'. There was no way
within Aristotelian logic that you could give a proper expression for
the logical form of such a proposition as 'Everyone loves someone',
let alone give an account of inferences involving such propositions.
Frege saw that one had to approach the question of generality in a
different way from Aristotle. We are to think of a proposition such
as 'Everyone loves someone' as the product of a two-stage process.
We begin by extracting from such propositions as 'John loves Mary',
the relational expression 'ξ loves η' where we may think of the Greek
letters 'ξ' and 'η' as gap-holders, showing where names are to be
inserted if we are to produce a proposition. As a first stage, we form
from this relational expression a predicate 'ξ loves someone', by
'binding' the second variable, the 'η'. We write the resulting predicate
in the form '$(\exists y)(\xi$ loves y)'. (I am using here, rather than Frege's own
notation, the Russellian notation that you will find in the *Tractatus*
itself.) You then as a second stage similarly 'bind' the 'ξ', to produce
the proposition: 'Given anyone, x say, then $(\exists y)(x$ loves y)', which we
write in the form '$(x)(\exists y)(x$ loves y)'. It is to be noted that if we had
reversed the stages of this process, we would have produced a
different proposition, with a different meaning: '$(\exists y)(x)(x$ loves y)'
– that means: 'There is someone who is loved by everyone'. Building
up propositions in stages in this manner will allow you to construct
propositions of arbitrary complexity, creating ever more logical
forms of propositions that go beyond anything that could be envisaged in Aristotelian logic. It was this advance that enabled Frege
single-handedly to transform logic from the trivialities of previous
logic to the powerful instrument that we know today.

He then laid down a set of axioms for his logic, to construct a
system within which we can provide rigorous proofs of truths of

logic. At the core of this system is a fragment that provides a complete axiomatization of what is now known as the first-order predicate calculus that has been the cornerstone of logic ever since.

The Foundations of Arithmetic is Frege's *philosophical* master-piece. He is concerned here to analyse the basic concepts of arith-metic, and above all to answer the question: 'What are numbers?' For our purposes, there are two points to note about this book. The first is that this is the work in which Frege introduces as one of his basic principles what is now called the 'Context Principle', which is given central significance in the *Tractatus*, and which we will look at in Section 3 (see discussion of 3.3). The second point is that in order to further his project of reducing arithmetic to logic, he identifies numbers with particular kinds of *sets* (in his terminology, 'exten-sions of concepts'). As a result, in his next work he will introduce axioms designed to incorporate a set theory into his logic. The way, however, that he does so leads to the difficulties that will introduce Russell into the picture.

Frege attempted the full implementation of his programme in *The Basic Laws of Arithmetic*: starting out from a few simple axioms and one rule of inference (*modus ponens*) he was to derive the truths of arithmetic as theorems of his system. These axioms were intended to be basic truths of logic, although Frege leaves it at an intuitive level that this is so. Most of them are trivialities whose status as logical truths no one would dispute (e.g., if p, then [if q then p]). However to carry through his programme he needed to add axioms that would incorporate a set theory into his logic. It was here that disaster struck. One axiom, Vb, can be shown to lead to a contra-diction. This axiom tells us that every concept has an extension, or in other words, given any property, there is a set whose members are all and only those things that possess that property. What Russell discovered was a way that this led to paradox, by considering the property of being a set that does not belong to itself. So we now turn to Russell.

Russell

Suppose we accept the intuitive idea of a set that is incorporated in Frege's axioms: that is, that given any concept there is a set whose members are precisely those things that fall under the concept. Now, some sets will belong to themselves, and others will not: thus, the set of all sets with more than ten members has more than ten members and so belongs to itself, but the set of all sets with fewer than ten members does not have fewer than ten members and so does *not* belong to itself.

We may therefore consider the concept of being a set that does not belong to itself. Frege's axioms guarantee the existence of the set whose members are all the sets that fall under that concept. Call this set **A**. We may then ask about **A**, whether it belongs to itself, or not. Assume that **A** does belong to itself. Then it must satisfy the condition for belonging to **A**. That is, it must be a set that does not belong to itself, which contradicts our assumption. Therefore **A** does not belong to itself. Therefore it does not satisfy the condition for belonging to itself: that is, it is not a set that does not belong to itself, which once again is a contradiction.

We must therefore reject Frege's axiom Vb, and produce a set theory that does not assume that given any property you can automatically move on to talk about the set of things possessing that property. Russell therefore set himself the task of repairing Frege's system, by modifying the set theory. The trick would be to find a principled way to weaken Frege's axioms sufficiently to avoid contradiction, while leaving them strong enough to be able to derive the truths of arithmetic from them.

The weakening of Frege's axioms was to be achieved by Russell's 'Theory of Types', something that will concern us in greater detail at the beginning of the 'Overview of Themes' chapter of this book. Frege's untrammelled set theory would be replaced by a set theory that was stratified. We would start out with individuals; then form sets of individuals (Sets of Type 1); sets whose members were all either individuals or sets of individuals (Sets of Type 2), and so on, with the rule that no set could contain members that were of the same or higher type than itself. Thus no set would belong to itself, and there could be no set of sets that do not belong to themselves, thus blocking Russell's Paradox.

The resulting axiomatic system, left like that, would no longer be able to generate the contradiction that Russell had discovered; but at the same time, thus weakened, it was no longer strong enough to prove all the required theorems of arithmetic. Russell therefore found it necessary to add three new axioms, to restore the strength necessary to the system, while leaving it free from paradox.

WITTGENSTEIN'S REACTIONS TO RUSSELL'S WORK

This is the point at which it is appropriate to introduce Wittgenstein himself into the story. Wittgenstein was dissatisfied with what Russell had done on two counts. One of these, his worries over the Theory of Types will concern us in the next chapter. The other worry was over the three additional axioms that Russell was forced to introduce – the 'Axiom of Reducibility', the 'Axiom of Infinity' and the 'Multiplicative Axiom'. Although these axioms gave Russell much of what he wanted, the question arose: 'What was the status of these axioms?' Were these axioms true? And, if they were true, were they truths *of logic*? That last question raised the further question: 'What did it amount to to say that something was or was not a truth of logic?'

Frege had left the question of what made his axioms truths of logic at a largely intuitive level, but at least they had the appearance of being such. Russell, however, had a wholly inadequate answer to this question (cf. the discussion of 6.1 of the *Tractatus* below), and introduced axioms purely to salvage his system, but whose claim to be true on logical grounds alone was completely suspect. If these axioms were *not* truths of logic, then of course the claim of Whitehead and Russell's *Principia Mathematica* to vindicate *logicism* was unfounded. The system of *Principia* would be just one mathematical axiomatic system alongside others.

Against this background, we may see Wittgenstein as embarking on the enquiry that would lead to the *Tractatus* with two initial questions: 'What were we to say about the Theory of Types?' and 'What account could we give of a truth of logic?', where the answer to the second question should make the unique status of truths of logic intelligible: both that they were necessary and that they were knowable *a priori*. It is to the first of these questions that we turn next.

CHAPTER 2

OVERVIEW OF THEMES

> Thus the aim of the book is to set a limit to thought, or rather – not to thought, but to the expression of thoughts: for to draw a limit to thought, we would have to be able to think both sides of this limit (and so we would have to be able to think what cannot be thought).
>
> The limit will therefore only be capable of being drawn in language, and what lies outside of the limit will be simply nonsense.[1]

Perhaps the best way to gain a preliminary overview of the *Tractatus* is to read the 'Author's Preface' carefully, and the two paragraphs just quoted in particular. Two questions immediately arise: 'What is meant here by a "limit" (or boundary [*Grenze*])?' and 'Why would one want to draw such a limit?'

To answer such questions we begin with the immediate context in which the *Tractatus* was written, and in particular, the *Tractatus* as a reaction to Russell's work. Russell had discovered a way of deriving the contradiction from the axioms of Frege's *Basic Laws* (Russell's Paradox) that we introduced in the preceding section – the set of all sets that did not belong to themselves belonged to itself if, and only if, it did not belong to itself. The interest of such logical paradoxes goes beyond their being intriguing puzzles; they are symptoms that we have a deep misunderstanding of some of our most basic ideas: if following up our intuitive understanding of those ideas can lead us into contradiction, we have radically to revise that intuitive understanding. Central to the task that Russell had set himself in *Principia Mathematica* was to repair Fregean logic: to find a principled response to his paradox. The aim was to show that, despite the appearances that were created by our intuitive understanding of the notion of a set, the offending sentence ('The set of all sets that do not belong to themselves belongs to itself') was meaningless. Basically he set about this by replacing our intuitive understanding of the notion of a set (given any property, there is a set whose members are precisely those things that possess that property) by a hierarchical conception, 'the Theory of Types'. With his hierarchical conception of sets went a hierarchical conception of predicates: no predicate could be significantly applied to entities of the wrong type. Nonsense would result from any attempt to construct a sentence, such as the paradoxical sentence that created the difficulty, in which one attempted to violate the type restrictions by applying a predicate to an entity of the wrong type.

One of the starting points for Wittgenstein's investigations that would lead eventually to the *Tractatus* was dissatisfaction with Russell's answer to the paradox, or rather to the way in which Russell had set out his answer to the paradox:

> 3.331 Russell's mistake is shown by the fact that he has to speak about the things his signs mean in drawing up his rules for them.

What is Wittgenstein's complaint? Why not talk about the things the signs mean in drawing the distinction between sense and nonsense? He later gives a clearer explanation than in the *Tractatus* itself:

> Grammatical conventions cannot be justified by describing what is represented. Any such description already presupposes the grammatical rules. That is to say, if anything is to count as nonsense in the grammar that is to be justified, then it cannot at the same time pass for sense in the grammar of the propositions that justify it (etc.).[2]

Russell wishes to say that if *fx* is a predicate that only takes arguments of a certain type and *a* is an entity of higher type than that, then '*fa*' will be nonsense. But that rapidly involves you in a curious kind of thumb-catching. Suppose we say that 'the set of individuals is an individual' is nonsense, and then say that this is because the predicate '*x* is an individual' is a predicate that is only applicable to individuals, and the set of individuals is not an individual. The final clause of our explanation turns out itself to be nonsense: we have violated the type restrictions we were trying to set up, in the very act of setting them up. It appears that any attempt to state the Theory of Types in the way Russell has done results in producing sentences that are condemned by the theory itself to be nonsensical. It is as though Russell is attempting to stand outside language and the world and look down on them from above, deciding where the boundary between sense and nonsense lay by seeing where language did, or did not, fit the world. Wittgenstein concluded that one had to remain resolutely *within* language and that there could not be such a thing as a *Theory* of Types: that what a Theory of Types attempted to say could not be *said* at all, but was something that was *shown* by the way language worked. To see how the paradoxical sentences were eliminated from the language, one would have to set about it in a completely different way from Russell. As Wittgenstein indicates at 3.33, the task would be to set up an account of logical syntax, an account of which sets of signs were propositions of the language, without at any point appealing as Russell had done to the meanings of those signs. If this were properly done, one would arrive at the result that Russell wished to achieve by a Theory of Types, but would get there by presenting a grammar for the language that would generate the propositions of the language without ever generating propositions that violated the type restrictions that Russell wanted to be observed. The resulting account of language would not *say* what Russell had said, but the structure of the language would *show* the structure that Russell wanted to *say* existed. In fact, the structure of the language would *mirror* the reality that the language was about.

My work has extended from the foundations of logic to the essence of the world.[3]

So far it may sound as if we were merely dealing with a technical question concerning the correct way to deal with logical paradoxes, but from the train of thought I have just sketched Wittgenstein drew a general moral that could eventually extend to the whole of metaphysics. Russell's Paradox arose because we misunderstood the way our language works, and if we understood the way our language works – if we had a correct account of logical syntax – then the paradox would be resolved, simply because a complete account of logical syntax would set the limits of language, not by stating what those limits were, but simply because the offending sentences would never be generated.

Wittgenstein therefore set himself the following ambitious programme. He would establish 'the general form of proposition': the general form of a variable that would range over every possible proposition. The general form of proposition would *show* the limits of language, since it would establish a systematic way of generating every possible proposition, and what could not be so generated would be thereby shown to be nonsense. This programme can be broken down into three stages: firstly, and most importantly, to discover the nature of propositions; secondly, to show that given the nature of propositions, there would have to be a general form of proposition; and thirdly, to carry out the technical task of specifying that general form.

PROPOSITIONS

Wittgenstein is guided by three basic principles:

1. 'To understand a proposition is to know what is the case if it is true' (4.024).
2. 'The logical constants do not stand in for anything' (4.0312).
3. 'Sense must be determinate' (3.23).

1. To understand a proposition is to know what is the case if it is true

This is the simplest of all the principles. Propositions are the kind of thing that could be true or false, right or wrong. Therefore they are quite different from names, where we could establish the meaning of a name by correlating the name with some existing feature in the world. If, however, propositions are to be true *or false*, then it must be possible to understand a proposition, without knowing whether it is true. We must therefore be able to understand a false proposition, not by seeing it as correlated with some actual feature in the world, but by seeing it as specifying the situation (*Sachlage*) that would make it true, independently of that situation actually existing: it must be possible to construct the situation that would make the proposition true from the proposition itself. But that is only possible if we can view the proposition as a **picture** or **model** of the situation that would make it true (4.01) – a picture (proposition) depicts reality by representing a situation, and depicts reality correctly or incorrectly (is true or false) according as that situation does or does not exist. In order that a picture should represent a situation, it must share a common logical form with that situation, have the same logical multiplicity as that situation (2.16, 4.04). The proposition does not, however, **say** that the situation has that form: it mirrors the form of the situation and in that way **shows** the logical form of reality.

2. The logical constants do not stand in for anything

The idea of a proposition as a picture or model seems to have relatively straightforward application to logically simple propositions. Let us consider a simple relational proposition, such as 'John loves Mary'. Here we may think of the name 'John' as standing in for the man John, the name 'Mary' for the woman Mary, and the fact that the names are related in a certain way (stand on opposite sides of the word 'loves') as representing the situation that John is related to Mary in a corresponding way. We should think in this way of the propositional sign, the sentence, not as a complex object, but as the **fact** that the signs in the sentence are related in a certain way.

That simple account, however, seems to leave us in the lurch when we think of the kind of logically complex propositions encountered all the time, such as: 'Once every four years, a president is elected in the USA'. Here it seems difficult to say in what way *this* proposition pictures the situation that makes it true. This is where the second basic principle in Wittgenstein's account of propositions comes in – 'the logical constants do not stand in for anything': the logical apparatus of the language – the words like 'and', 'not', 'all' and 'some' function in a way that is radically different from names. We may intuitively contrast the logically simple proposition 'John loves Mary' with the logically complex proposition 'John loves Mary or Kate'. We are to think of the first proposition as modelling a state of affairs, and as being true if that state of affairs exists – if there is a **fact** that John loves Mary. But 'John loves Mary or Kate' is either made true by the existence of the fact that John loves Mary, or by existence of the fact that John loves Kate. It is not made true by the existence of a 'disjunctive fact', that John loves Mary or Kate. We could only talk of such disjunctive facts if in fact 'or' stood in for a feature of that fact in the way that 'John' and 'Mary' stand in for features of the state of affairs of John loving Mary. We must therefore think of the logical apparatus as having a completely different rôle from the other elements of the language. Its function is to build up

logically complex propositions out of logically simple propositions –
elementary propositions – and a logically complex proposition pictures a logically complex situation in virtue of the fact that the
logical apparatus gives to the proposition the same logical multiplicity as the logically complex situation it represents – it must give
to the proposition the capacity to pick out precisely which combinations of simple states of affairs must obtain for us to say that the
logically complex situation obtains. The way in which logically
complex propositions are built up out of elementary propositions is
truth-functional. That is to say, we specify the sense of a complex
proposition by saying which combinations of truth and falsity of
elementary propositions make it true, and which, false. The key
thesis is, therefore, that *every proposition is a truth-function of elementary propositions*.

3. Sense must be determinate

So far, we have elementary propositions that can be formulated
without any use of logical apparatus and which model simple states
of affairs, and the sense of any other proposition is to be explained
as a truth-function of such elementary propositions. Complication
arises because the apparent logical form of a proposition need not
be its real one (4.0031): we cannot tell from the surface-grammatical
form of a proposition what its real logical form may be. We need a
criterion for deciding what is, and what is not, an elementary proposition. Here is where the 'demand for determinacy of sense' (3.23)
comes in. The propositions that we ordinarily encounter are all more
or less specific, but the world is absolutely specific: our propositions
are always made true or false by the utterly specific concrete situations that we actually encounter. Therefore a correct account of the
sense of a proposition must show how it is made true by the detailed
nitty-gritty of the world: how unspecific propositions are related to
the specific situations the world offers us. We therefore break our
unspecific propositions down into truth-functions of utterly specific
propositions, each of which picks out a simple, utterly specific state
of affairs and is made true by the existence of that state of affairs.
The criterion then for an elementary proposition is complete specificity, its picking out exactly one simple state of affairs. States of
affairs are then seen as 'combinations of **objects**' (2.01) and obtain if
and only if the objects are appropriately combined, where the
objects are argued to be **simple** and to 'form the substance of the

world' (2.021) since they are common to every world we could possibly imagine. (It is important here not to prejudge the question what examples of such objects would be: the most we can say at the outset is that they are features of reality that could be referred to by name.) We are to think of the world as 'the totality of facts' (1.1), as determined by which states of affairs exist and which do not. A proposition is then true or false if and only if it is answerable to the world, that is to say, if it picks out precisely those combinations of states of affairs which must exist if it is to be true.

THE EXISTENCE OF A GENERAL FORM OF PROPOSITION

Although it is a crucial step in the argument of the book, Wittgenstein presents his argument for there being such a general form only in a very compressed form at 4.5. The core of the argument is that if it is possible to understand a proposition independently of knowing what is the case, it must derive its meaning from its position within the system of language. Therefore there must be a system of language; a system that recursively generates every significant proposition of the language.

SPECIFYING THE GENERAL FORM OF PROPOSITION

In section 5 of the *Tractatus*, Wittgenstein then constructs the general form of proposition, starting out from the idea that every proposition is a truth-function of elementary propositions. The task here is twofold. First he must devise a piece of apparatus that will enable him to generate every truth-function of elementary propositions in a uniform manner. Second, he must show that this apparatus is capable of handling the whole of standard Fregean logic. The first task is achieved by the introduction of the '**N-operator**' – an operator which, applied to a range of propositions, will produce a proposition that is true if and only if all those propositions are false (5.502). Sheffer had shown that 'neither . . . nor . . .' was a connective that was powerful enough to handle the whole of elementary (propositional) logic. Wittgenstein's N-operator is the infinite analogue of this, which was capable of dealing with cases where we wished to construct truth-functions of infinitely many propositions. Wittgenstein then indicates how he would treat Fregean logic by showing how to use this operator to explain general propositions

(5.52) and identity propositions (5.532). He has thereby shown (1) how the whole of Fregean logic can be presented using only truth-functional apparatus and (2) how to present the general form of proposition, by representing all propositions as the result of successive applications of the N-operator to elementary propositions.

TRUTHS OF LOGIC

Wittgenstein's second major cause of dissatisfaction with Russell's work was Russell's account of logical truth. Russell explained truths of logic as true, completely general, propositions (propositions void of any particular content whatever). For Wittgenstein this account completely failed to capture the most basic feature of our conception of a truth of logic: its necessity. Wittgenstein insisted that the truths of logic were **tautologies** (6.1): propositions that said nothing: if a proposition of logic was true independently of the way the world was, it told us nothing about the world. Since we do not need to appeal to the world to settle its truth value, the proposition itself must contain all the information necessary to decide that it is true, and in an adequate notation we would be able to recognize that a proposition was a truth of logic by simple inspection. The cost of the necessity of the truths of logic is their utter vacuity. Wittgenstein explains this by seeing them as degenerate cases of truth-functions of elementary propositions, propositions that are true no matter what combination of truth and falsity of the elementary propositions we consider. They are still part of the language: they are *senseless* but not *nonsense* (4.461).

THE LIMITS OF LANGUAGE

The general form of proposition sets the limits of language by encompassing every possible significant proposition. What lies on the other side of the limit will simply be nonsense. At the same time, the structure of language will form a 'great mirror' (5.511) reflecting the structure of the world and showing 'the essence of the world' (5.4711). Any attempt to *say* what is thereby shown results in nonsense. (Metaphysics in particular is the attempt to convert what is shown into a theory of the world.) Paradoxically, at 6.54 Wittgenstein will conclude by claiming that anyone who understands him will also recognize the propositions of his own book to be nonsense.

CHAPTER 3

READING THE *TRACTATUS*

Most readers when they first attempt to read the *Tractatus* react with complete bewilderment. The initial obscurity of the text, even by comparison with other major philosophical texts, is extraordinary. For the majority of readers, when they first open the book, the impression is of a set of aphorisms, many of which are completely unintelligible. Even for those remarks where it is apparently clear enough what is being claimed, it is frequently unclear why Wittgenstein is making these claims – they often appear to be asserted without any attempt at justification, and the point of the claims is equally obscure. It may even be unclear what the book is meant to be about. However, although the *Tractatus* is a difficult book, it is not nearly as inaccessible as that initial impression would suggest. At its core is a remarkably simple account of the relation of language to reality, and that at least, together with Wittgenstein's arguments for it, can be readily grasped. The difficulties and complexities of the text all lie in the further ramifications and implications that Wittgenstein draws from that simple account. But even if the *Tractatus* never becomes an easy book to read, much of the initial difficulty in approaching the text can be alleviated if you bear in mind the following points:

- The first, and most important, point is to understand the layout of the book, and the way in which the numbering system is meant to work. Wittgenstein himself gives a brief explanation of this in the footnote to the first proposition of the text, but it is worth spelling out in full, and appreciating its significance for the way in which the book is intended to be read. The *Tractatus* was not composed, and is not supposed to be read in the way in which one normally reads a book, with its paragraphs arranged in a linear sequence. You may, instead, understand the way it *is* organized if you think of it as arranged in a tree-like structure with the seven main propositions, numbered 1 to 7, set out at the top of the tree. These propositions, read in consecutive order, give one, in broadest outline, the overall trajectory of the argument of the book. This broad outline is then elaborated and filled-in in the following way. We now add branches downwards, the paragraphs numbered with only one decimal place (1.1, 1.2, 2.1, 2.2, 3.1 . . .), arranging them with 1.1 and 1.2 branching off proposition 1 as the principal comments on 1, and so forth. This will give the reader a second version of the argument of the book filled-in in greater detail than the first, either presenting arguments for, or giving explanations of, or drawing consequences from, the main thesis. You then repeat the process until you arrive at the whole account that Wittgenstein is arguing for in full detail. One way of presenting this would be to set up the *Tractatus* as a hypertext, and indeed there is a hypertext version of the *Tractatus* to be found on the web at <http://www.kfs.org/~jonathan/witt>.

You can see the consequence of this unorthodox layout if you look at 4.016 and 4.02. If you attempt to read the book in its apparent linear order we seem to be told that there is no essential difference between a hieroglyphic script and a normal alphabetic script, and that we could see this from the fact that we could understand the sense of a propositional sign without having to have it explained to us. One may then well be perplexed as to what Wittgenstein's train of thought is here. However, in the order dictated by the number system, 4.02 does not immediately follow 4.016 but follows 4.01 – 4.011 to 4.016 are simply comments on 4.01 interpolated between 4.01 and 4.02. This means that the 'We can see this . . .' of 4.02 refers to a sentence that occurred at a place that was more than a page of text earlier. Now we can see that Wittgenstein is claiming that we can see that a proposition is a picture of reality from the fact that we can understand its sense without having it explained to us, which is an idea that he will then elaborate in the paragraphs that follow 4.02.

In this way, one must learn to trace Wittgenstein's lines of thought by following through the paths indicated by the number system and not simply by following the sentences as they occur on the page. The number system is not infallible – there are a number of remarks that seem to be inserted as best they can be in the overall structure, not because that is their proper place within that structure, but because they were remarks that Wittgenstein wished to retain but lacked an obvious place for within the text, and that he therefore inserted as best he could. But even if it is not infallible, once you get used to tracking the numbers, it generally provides helpful guidance as to the correct way to trace Wittgenstein's thought, and it is always worth asking yourself why a given paragraph is placed where it is.

• The *Tractatus* is sometimes thought to be a book in which we are presented with a series of aphorisms, presented on a take-it-or-leave-it basis and without any hard argument to back them up. The opposite is the case. There is a great deal of argument for the positions Wittgenstein presents, but the text is extraordinarily compressed, so that he will characteristically simply indicate the line along which the argument would go and leave it to the reader to fill in the details. Consider for instance the opening sentence of 4.021:

> A proposition is a picture of reality: for, if I understand the proposition, I know the situation it represents.

It is clear both that Wittgenstein has an argument in mind here, and that the argument at this point is crucial to the whole development of the book. It is also clear that in most philosophical texts we should expect such an argument to be fleshed out in full detail. Paradoxically, the text appears to be particularly compressed and elusive in the case of some of the most crucial stages in the argument, such as 2.02–2.0212, 3.23–3.24 and 5.62–5.64. Both Russell and Ramsey urged him to spell out the arguments in full, but he strenuously resisted their advice. There may have been a number of reasons for this, including a purely aesthetic one. But that aesthetic reason may also have had a philosophical point: he was interested in communicating an overall system of thought that might have been lost if the text was cluttered with detailed argument. It is also the case that many of the claims he makes are justified not so much by particular arguments that can be presented at this stage as by the position of those claims within the overall story that he is telling. It must be confessed that there are also a few places where it looks very much as if some of his claims are made on purely intuitive grounds, and that he himself would have found it difficult or even impossible to spell out his arguments for adopting them.

Above all, however, Wittgenstein wants and expects a readership prepared to engage actively with his text, to enter into the spirit of his enterprise by seeing for themselves why he says what he says, and to work out without being told what the underlying argument is. This means that if you are to benefit from reading the *Tractatus*, you cannot do so without being willing to think through for yourself the positions Wittgenstein is presenting. Even more than with other philosophical texts, coming to understand the text involves readers in a philosophical exploration for themselves, thinking through for themselves the issues he is dealing with.

In the sections that follow, I shall be paying particular attention to those arguments where, although they are crucial for the whole book, Wittgenstein's presentation of those arguments is extraordinarily compressed.

- There is also another respect in which Wittgenstein makes things difficult for the reader, and this remained true throughout his life from the *Tractatus* to the *Philosophical Investigations*. It is characteristic of all Wittgenstein's writings that he does not tell the reader where he is coming from. He always writes in such a way as to assume a readership that is already concerned about the issues and complex of problems that his work addresses, even when these issues are quite unlike many of the issues with which most philosophers have been traditionally concerned. This is particularly true in the case of the *Tractatus*, where he presupposes an interest in and knowledge of the work of Frege and Russell, and a concern with the issues with which they were concerned, even though at the time at which he wrote the book, Frege was still virtually unknown to the general philosophical community. It is, as a result, important in gaining a preliminary orientation in the *Tractatus* that you first have an awareness of the general outlines of the issues with which Frege and Russell were dealing in order to place Wittgenstein's *Tractatus* in its appropriate context. A large number of the remarks are either endorsement of, elaborations of, or criticisms of positions that had been put forward by one of the two. In the course of this book, we shall have occasion to look at some of the specific ideas of both Frege and Russell that Wittgenstein is reacting to. But at the outset, you should bear in mind the general issues that concerned them. Here I shall simply list some of the questions that were, for

Wittgenstein, raised by their work, and which would form at least the starting point for his enquiry: What is logic, and what is it for a proposition to be a truth of logic? What account are we to give of the 'logical constants' – the apparatus of logic: words like 'and', 'or', 'not', 'some' and 'all'? What is a proposition? What is it for a proposition to be true? How does a proposition relate to reality? What is the nature of the linguistic complexity of a proposition, and how is its meaning related to the meanings of the words of which it is composed? How do we give an account of the way language works in such a way that the logical paradoxes, such as Russell's Paradox, do not arise? We can go a long way to understanding the *Tractatus* by seeing a major part of Wittgenstein's undertaking as an attempt to replace Russell's answers to such questions with something better.

• One important resource for coming to terms with the *Tractatus* is the various writings contained in the book edited by G.H. von Wright and G.E.M. Anscombe as 'Ludwig Wittgenstein, *Notebooks 1914–1916*', but it is a resource that must be handled with care. It is never safe to find a remark in the *Notebooks* and simply assume that Wittgenstein continued to hold what was said there when he finally wrote the *Tractatus* itself. Not only is there considerable development in his thinking during the writing of these earlier notes, so that much of what he says there will have been rejected and superseded by the time he wrote the *Tractatus*, but also a large number of the remarks have an experimental or ephemeral status, where Wittgenstein is trying out an idea. These earlier writings must be regarded as work in progress, and although they can be useful aids in understanding the completed work, they are far from infallible pointers to how that work will be completed.

To understand the right way to use the *Notebooks* as a guide to understanding the *Tractatus*, it is helpful to consider the way in which Wittgenstein composed his book. Throughout his life, his method of writing a book was what is called '*Zettelschrift*'. He would regularly write the ideas as they occurred to him in the form of short paragraphs; he would then select those paragraphs that he wished to retain in the final work and polish them until they were in a form that finally satisfied him. He would then arrange these paragraphs in a coherent sequence to produce the final book. In the case of the *Tractatus*, it looks as if he started out with the seven main propositions, labelled 1 to 7, and the remaining paragraphs are, for the most part, selections from pre-existing material arranged to fit into that skeletal structure. But our immediate concern is that what this means is that a considerable number of the paragraphs in the *Tractatus* occur either directly in, or in an earlier version of, the *Notebooks*.

Because of this, a large number of propositions in the *Tractatus* had originally appeared in a different context from the one in which they stand in the *Tractatus* itself. Seeing those remarks in their original context can frequently be a guide to the correct way to interpret them: though it must be borne in mind that sometimes there will be in that surrounding context remarks that Wittgenstein would no longer subscribe to when he finally wrote the *Tractatus*, and as a result it can even be that a proposition that is preserved in the *Tractatus* will have a slightly different significance for Wittgenstein from that which it had when he originally wrote it.

By browsing the highly desultory notes that Wittgenstein made, you can gain a preliminary insight into many of the problems that Wittgenstein wanted to confront. In particular it is worth reading through the first appendix to the *Notebooks*: 'Notes on Logic, 1913', to gain an understanding of the concerns that motivated the enquiry leading up to the *Tractatus*. For an excellent example of the way in which the *Notebooks* can assist one in understanding the *Tractatus* we may consider the discussion running from p. 59 through to p. 71. A version of *Tractatus* 3.24 occurs at p. 69 of this discussion. Proposition 3.24 is extraordinarily compressed, with considerable unclarity as to what Wittgenstein meant by 'determinacy of sense', or why he is demanding it. Reading through the earlier discussion, without necessarily maintaining that Wittgenstein would subscribe to the detail of what he was saying in these notes, provides a crucial entry point to 3.24 itself.

The golden rule, however, is: never ascribe a view to Wittgenstein on the basis of a remark in the *Notebooks*, unless you can find corroboration of that view, either direct or indirect, in the text of the *Tractatus* itself.

- The logical notation used in the *Tractatus* is that of *Principia Mathematica*. Most of its features are still in use today ('v' = 'or'; '~' = 'It is not the case that'; '⊃' = 'if . . . then'; '($\exists x$) . . .' =

'There is an x such that . . .', and '(x) . . .' = 'For all x . . .'). But there is one feature of the *Principia* notation that may be unfamiliar, and confusing. This is the use of the full stop both as a bracket and as the sign for 'and'. In this Guide, when not actually quoting Wittgenstein, I have substituted for this the more familiar '&' for 'and', and brackets where necessary.

SECTION 1. 'THE WORLD IS EVERYTHING THAT IS THE CASE'

The initial questions raised by the short introductory section of the Tractatus *are: 'Why, in a book devoted to questions concerning the nature of logic and language, and whose central aim is to "draw a limit to thinking" does Wittgenstein begin with a characterization of the world?' and 'In what way do these opening paragraphs set the scene for what is to follow?' The world as the totality of facts: What is the notion of 'fact' here? Is this a 'metaphysics of facts'? The stress throughout this passage on absolute generality and exhaustiveness; does it make sense to talk of such a totality?; the world as 'dividing' into facts.*

The *Tractatus* opens, in the short first section of the book, with a highly abstract characterization of the world. This is then continued in the initial part of the second section with a more detailed discussion of the states of affairs whose existence and non-existence we have been told in the first section constitute the world. This part of the book – from 1 to 2.063 – is clearly intended to set the scene for what follows, and the first question that needs addressing before we look at the detail of what is said in these remarks is the following: 'Why, in a book that is concerned with the nature of logic and propositions, and whose purpose is claimed to be to "set the limits of language", does Wittgenstein begin by talking, not about these topics, but apparently about something completely different, and present us with what initially at least looks like a metaphysical worldview?'

Three points help clarify this question. It is necessary here to anticipate ideas that we shall encounter as we progress through the book, so that some of the points made will only become clearer later, but we introduce them at this stage to give the reader a preliminary orientation in approaching these opening paragraphs of the *Tractatus*. Our aim is to indicate the rôle of these paragraphs, so as to explain some of their features, and, indeed, what they are doing in the book at all.

The basic concept guiding Wittgenstein's whole enquiry is the concept of truth, or rather, being true or false. This is so, whether he is concerned with the nature of propositions, the nature of logic, or the distinction between the significant use of language and nonsense. A proposition is essentially that which is true or false; a truth of logic is a proposition that is true no matter what is the case; and an apparent proposition is nonsensical if you cannot give a coherent account of the conditions under which it would be true or false.

In this way, the central question becomes: 'What is it for a proposition to be true, or false, the right or wrong thing to say?' But to be true or false, right or wrong, is to be answerable to something that sets the standard for rightness and wrongness. The world is introduced here simply as the sum total of that which sets the standard for rightness and wrongness for the propositions of our language, and so the task of the book will then be to answer the question: 'What is the nature of the relation of the propositions of our language to the world conceived in the way set out here, so that they are true or false according to the way the world is?' We thereby implicitly draw 'the limits of language', in the sense that if someone puts forward an apparent proposition, where it can be shown that they can give no coherent account of the way in which their putative proposition stands in such a relation to the world as thus conceived, then they have transgressed the limits of language and they have failed to give any meaning to their apparent proposition.

With this in mind, we can gain a preliminary understanding of the following points about these introductory paragraphs:

1. The world as that to which our thought and language is answerable

A world of facts, not things
If the world is to be presented as that to which all that we say and think is answerable, it is as a world of facts, not as a world that is simply an inventory of the things that the world contains. If 'John is happy' is true, it is not made true simply by John, but by the state of John – the fact that he is happy. One can think of the *Tractatus*, initially at least, as an attempt to give a systematic and disciplined working out of the intuitive idea that a proposition is true if and only if it corresponds with the facts. When, however, people talk of 'Correspondence *Theories* of Truth', they frequently have in mind the idea that corresponding to every true proposition there is exactly one fact that makes the proposition true. The Achilles heel of *such*

theories has always been the impossibility of specifying in any plausible manner such a fact for all but a small range of highly special propositions. Wittgenstein, by contrast, is retaining the plural 'facts', and is attempting to show how any given proposition can be shown to be answerable to the vast battery of facts that constitute the world.

Generality

There is a stress in these opening paragraphs on absolute generality – *everything* that is the case, the *totality* of facts, *all* the facts. This is important in a number of respects. Firstly, what Wittgenstein is after is a completely general account of propositions and of truth and falsity that will be applicable to any proposition regardless of its subject matter. Slightly differently, the account of the world is intended not to prejudge any metaphysical issues whatever. Here, the world is everything of whatever sort there is that is the case – everything to which our thought and speech is addressed. Read this way, the stress on everything that is the case is intended to leave open such questions as whether the world is to be conceived in idealist or realist terms: in so far as there is anything to talk about, and which makes what we say true or false, such facts are to be included in the world. The characterization of the world here is meant to be acceptable to all the parties in any of the standard metaphysical disputes.

The other main point of the stress on the totality of the facts is that it is the world conceived in this way that can set the limits to language, to what can be said (leaving unclarified at this stage what is meant by talking of 'limits' here). It is because the world is everything that is the case that Wittgenstein can say: 'Logic fills the world: the limits of the world are also its limits' (5.61). If an apparent proposition cannot be shown to be answerable to the world, conceived in this way, then we can give no coherent account of what it would be for it to be true or false, and it is thereby exposed as not a genuine proposition at all, but simply nonsense.

Minimalism

The characterization of the world occupies less than half a page of text, and its further elaboration in paragraphs 2–2.063 less than four further pages. Everything is left at a highly schematic level, in which, when Wittgenstein talks of 'facts', 'state of affairs' and 'objects', he offers us no examples of what such would actually be. We are not told for instance whether objects would be some kind of material atoms – Newtonian point-masses – or immediate objects of experience – sense data, say. We are also not told whether the term 'objects' will cover simply particulars or whether it will include universals, or properties or relations, or even whether 'objects' are such that they cannot be characterized as particular or universal. The most that we are told are some formal requirements that the objects must satisfy: they are simple, they are common to every world we could imagine, and they combine together to form states of affairs. This has led a number of commentators to speculate as to what examples he would have had in mind. What Wittgenstein says at 5.557–5.5571 shows that all such speculation is misconceived. The account he is putting forward requires that there should be simple objects and states of affairs, but *what* they are could not be settled by the kind of logical investigation that he is undertaking. To discover *that*, we would have to go beyond such an investigation and look at what Wittgenstein in 5.557 calls 'the application of logic', which would be some sort of empirical exploration of the way our language actually works – most plausibly this would consist in actually carrying through the programme of analysis envisaged in the *Tractatus*. What we can say is that if we consider the requirements that Wittgenstein lays down for his objects, they would have to be very different from the tiny particles that we first think of when we hear the phrase 'simple objects'. If the book can be considered to be advocating a form of atomism, it is '*logical* atomism', and not some form of physical atomic theory. We shall look in the next section at what sort of alternatives would be more appropriate candidates, and only remark here that some of the candidates that have been offered – such as immediate objects of experience – seem very difficult to reconcile with the conditions Wittgenstein lays down for his objects.

But if Wittgenstein's account of the world is meant to leave open many of the traditional 'metaphysical' questions about the world, it is also no part of his purpose to introduce a 'metaphysics' of his own in these opening paragraphs of the book. How far he succeeds in this may be a matter of dispute: it certainly *looks* as if he is advocating a metaphysical atomism, and many of his claims here look like substantial metaphysical claims. We may mention a couple of the most obvious examples: there is the claim that there is a set of simple objects that are common to every world we could possibly imagine, and there is also the claim that it is possible to break the world down into a set of *independent* facts. It is, however, important to bear in mind how little we are told about the objects, and the reader should postpone deciding the extent to which these do represent genuine metaphysical commitments until it is decided how such claims are to be interpreted. It is at any rate safe to say that, rightly or wrongly, Wittgenstein himself did not intend to develop a metaphysics in these opening sections, and in an important sense, these opening paragraphs are meant to be read in a way that is as vacuous as possible: this is as much as can be said about the world without begging *any* questions as to its detailed nature.

2. Realism or idealism?

The full force of this point will only become clear as the *Tractatus* progresses, but it should be borne in mind even at this stage, if you are properly to appreciate what is going on in these introductory paragraphs. The book will develop an account of language in such a way as to show how the propositions of language are true or false according to the way the world is, and to show significant language as answerable to the world. One of the central themes of the book is the idea that a proposition must have something in common – a form or 'logical multiplicity' – with the situation it represents for it to be possible for a proposition to be a representation of that situation at all (see, e.g., 2.16, 4.04, 4.12). Further, Wittgenstein will argue that not only must an individual proposition have something in common with the situation that it represents, but that the structure of language as a whole must reflect the structure of the world, so that at 5.11 he will talk of logic as 'the great mirror' (see also 6.13), and at 5.4711, he writes:

> To give the essence of proposition means to give the essence of all description, *and hence* the essence of the world. (my italics)

As a result, there is an extensive parallelism between the claims made about the world in these introductory paragraphs and the claims that will subsequently be made about language, and a considerable number of these opening paragraphs will find an echo in later paragraphs, with apparently 'ontological' remarks being mirrored by corresponding 'linguistic' remarks. Thus, to give a few examples: at 1.21, we are told that the world divides into a set of independent facts, and later we will be told that language can be built up out of a set of logically independent elementary propositions (see, e.g., 4.211); states of affairs are combinations of objects (2.01), and propositions are concatenations of names (4.22); such objects are simple (2.02), and names are simple signs (3.202); we cannot conceive of objects independently of the possibility of their combining with other objects to form states of affairs (2.0121), and a name only has meaning in the context of a proposition (3.3).

This seems inevitably to prompt the question: 'Does language have to have a certain structure in common with the world in order that it should be possible for it to make claims about a world with that structure, or, on the other hand, is the structure ascribed to the world in these opening paragraphs no more than a structure that has been imposed upon it by the linguistic forms of language?' And that question seems to lead straightforwardly to two possible interpretations, which we may label a 'realist' reading of the text, and a 'transcendental idealist' reading. According to the first, the world would have a pre-existing structure, independently of our thinking and talking about it and it is because the world has such a structure that any language that is to engage with the world must have a corresponding structure. According to the second, we have no access to the world and what it is like independently of our linguistic representations of the world, and the structure that we ascribe to the world – all this talk of states of affairs and objects – are no more than shadows cast by the forms of our language; what the world is like 'in itself' is something that is necessarily beyond our grasp, possibly having a completely different structure, or even no structure at all. Some version of both readings have been advocated by various commentators, and it seems at first possible to give a consistent reading of the text either adopting a realist or an idealist interpretation of Wittgenstein's remarks. What is more, at different stages of the development it sometimes seems natural to see Wittgenstein as arguing from the nature of language to the nature of the world, and at other times more natural to see the argument as running in the opposite direction.

The questions just raised occur quite naturally, and it is important that the reader should have them in mind when reading the book. Wittgenstein's own position, however, if I have understood him aright, is to argue that in the end, the two alternatives canvassed are unreal, and that the very raising of these questions represents an unwitting attempt on the reader's part to make 'logic transgress the limits of the world' – an impossible attempt that can only result in speaking nonsense. We will return to this when we look at what is undoubtedly the most difficult, but crucial, sequence in the whole book, the discussion of solipsism in the 5.6s. For now, I just remark that one of the main points of the concluding remark of that sequence – that 'solipsism strictly carried through coincides with pure realism' – is precisely a rejection of the idea that the alternatives canvassed in the preceding paragraph were real. However inescapable it might appear that we decide between these two apparently incompatible readings, and hence that the questions raised seemed urgent and of fundamental importance, Wittgenstein wishes to persuade us that, despite appearances, we have actually given no sense to them.

3. The problematic nature of the remarks of the Tractatus

The final point to be aware of before we turn to the detail of what is said in the opening paragraphs is again one whose full significance will only emerge as we work through the *Tractatus*, and in this case is a point that can only be properly addressed right at the end of this guide. There is something profoundly problematic about the enterprise Wittgenstein is inviting us to engage in with him, and he will notoriously say at 6.54: 'My propositions are elucidatory in this way: anyone who understands me finally recognizes them as nonsense . . . '. There are several distinguishable trains of thought that lead to this paradoxical conclusion, which I shall detail when we come to look at 6.54 itself, but here we may consider two that are immediately relevant even at this introductory stage. The first is the idea that if our enterprise is to show how language fits the world, then what we would like to do is to describe the facts in the world and the propositions that are made true by those facts, and show the fit between them – and that apparently is what Wittgenstein is proceeding to do. The only way, however, to describe the facts that make a given proposition true is to use precisely the same form of words as is used in the proposition (or at best a logically equivalent proposition), so that we end up saying: ' "It is raining" is made true by the fact that it is raining', which is scarcely the startling news we wanted. Wittgenstein is apparently attempting the impossible: adopting a vantage-point above language and the world, and describing the relation between them as seen from that perspective, which would require that 'we should be able to place ourselves with propositions beyond logic, that is, beyond the world' (4.12) and 'what we cannot think we cannot think, and so we cannot say what we cannot think' (5.61). In this way we finally recognize that the sentences we uttered in trying to describe that relation were in fact sentences to which no meaning could be given. The other, related, point is that it will prove to be impossible to speak meaningfully about the world as a whole (see 6.45), and that we cannot say such things as: 'These are all the facts there are', or 'These are all the objects [or e.g. propositions] there are'. But he in fact apparently begins by doing precisely that: 'The world is determined by the facts, and by their being *all* the facts'. At this point there emerges a fundamental disagreement between Wittgenstein and Russell that we shall look at when we come to discuss Wittgenstein's treatment of general propositions at 5.52. For Russell, a complete specification of the world would consist in specifying all the particular facts (in Wittgenstein's terminology the existence and non-existence of states of affairs), together with a general fact, namely the fact that these were all the particular facts there were. But for Wittgenstein, there was no such fact; there were only the particular facts. But that means that to try to talk of 'the totality of facts' must result in nonsense. What Wittgenstein is doing in putting himself in such a paradoxically self-stultifying position will form the topic for the final section of this study. But at the outset, there are two points for the reader to bear in mind: (1) however we understand it, the problematic nature of the remarks that Wittgenstein is making in the *Tractatus* is not an accidental feature, but one of the central points of the book. Therefore, if you are to come to terms with Wittgenstein's enterprise, you should be sensitive while reading to the paradoxical nature of the propositions of the *Tractatus*: the way in which they continually imply the impossibility of saying what they are apparently saying. (2) The second point is the converse of the first. If you are to understand Wittgenstein, there is no alternative to reading the propositions of the *Tractatus* as if they were straightforward claims. It is only after you have worked through the book that you can seriously address the question: 'What are we to make of Wittgenstein's claim that his own propositions are nonsense?'

Against this background we may look at the content of the paragraphs of the first section, where there are two main paragraphs to comment on: (1) 1.1: the contrast between the world as the totality of facts, and as the totality of things, and (2) 1.2: the idea of the world as 'dividing' into a set of *independent* facts.

A world of facts

At 1.1 Wittgenstein sets up a contrast between the world as a world of facts and the world as a world of things. The initial reason for this contrast is clear enough: you do not specify the world by giving an inventory of the objects it contains. To know what the world is like, you have to know how things are arranged: the mere list of objects is compatible with a variety of ways the world might have been in addition to the way it actually is. If the world is everything that is the case, that is everything with which we can possibly be concerned in our thought and speech, and is that to which everything we say is answerable, then what we say is answerable not to objects, but to the facts of the case.

But alongside this, there is a second, related concern in these opening paragraphs. Wittgenstein himself explains 1.1 later as follows:

> The world does not consist of a catalogue of things and facts about them (like the catalogue of a show) . . . What the world is is given by description and not by a list of objects.[1]

The point about the catalogue of the show is that it is not as if we are first aware of things and then facts about those things. The only access we have to things is our knowledge of facts about them, and those things are being seen by Wittgenstein as essentially potential elements of states of affairs (see 2.012). Wittgenstein is in fact assigning a fundamental role to what is called the 'Context Principle' in all his thinking about objects: objects are the references of names, and those names only have meaning in the context of a proposition. We shall look at this in detail at 3.3, but for now we can say that the spirit of Wittgenstein's account is that we do not first start out with a notion of an object, and arrive at a notion of a fact by treating objects as building blocks out of which we build facts; rather, we arrive at the notion of an object by analysing facts.

But to take the opening paragraphs of the *Tractatus* seriously, we have to take the idea of facts as features of the world seriously. Many philosophers have regarded taking the idea of facts thus seriously with suspicion: saying that it is a fact that *p* is, it is claimed, no more than a circumlocution for saying that *p*, and even, curiously, that facts are true propositions.[2] It is, however, indisputable that there are not only things, but ways in which things are arranged, and if we wish to know whether a given proposition is true, we must attend not to what things there are but their arrangements and state – we must examine the facts on the ground. The indisputable fact that: 'it is a fact that *p*' is equivalent to '*p*' is no more surprising, and no more makes facts unreal, than the fact that it is indisputable that 'John' names John, makes John unreal. It simply goes without saying that we use precisely the same words for a piece of language as to describe what that piece of language is about.

The real issues are not whether there are ways things are, and ways they are arranged. The proper question lies elsewhere. If we accept that there are facts, are we to think of facts as complex objects composed of the things that the facts are about? When Wittgenstein first showed the *Tractatus* to Frege, Frege seems to have assumed that it was Wittgenstein's intention to think of facts as such complex objects. Wittgenstein is reported to have been irritated by Frege's comments at the time, but ten years later, he seems to have thought that they had some cogency.[3] It is difficult to sort out what is the truth of the matter here, but the evidence suggests that Wittgenstein's first reaction was closer to the mark. Frege had not made a detailed study of the *Tractatus*; his comments may have been based on a relatively superficial impression of the book, and Wittgenstein's later recollections of his earlier ideas are never wholly reliable. At the time Wittgenstein, indeed, contrasted facts and complexes,[4] and did not talk in the *Tractatus* itself in the ways assumed by Frege's criticism – specifically he does not talk about the objects as parts of the facts that concern them. If Wittgenstein was confused it was on another, related matter: what in the *Notebooks* he called 'the theory of the complex': the idea that if it is true that John loves Mary, then there would exist a complex [*John-loving-Mary*].[5] This was different from the fact that John loves Mary: and it is to the theory of the complex, and also to his assumption that everyday complex objects such as human beings could be considered as 'complexes' in this sense, rather than his conception of the world as a world of facts, that his later criticisms are directed. By the time of the *Tractatus* the 'theory of the complex' has largely disappeared from Wittgenstein's thinking, although it seems to make a guest appearance at 2.0201, when we shall return to it. But even when complexes are mentioned in the *Tractatus*, they are always presented as disappearing under analysis, and although I shall explain the argument at 2.02–2.03 with reference to the theory of the complex, since I believe that is more faithful to Wittgenstein's thinking, it would be perfectly possible to spell out that argument in terms of everyday complex objects rather than Wittgensteinian complexes.

There are several reasons for refusing to regard facts as complex objects, and for believing that it was not Wittgenstein's intention so to regard them:

- In the first place, and most fundamentally, if you make a fact out to be an object – a thing composed of simpler things – then you betray the insight which led Wittgenstein to invite us to see the world as the totality of facts and not of things. If we are insisting that our propositions are answerable to facts and not things, we miss the point of that insistence if we then, in turn, simply regard those facts as just another kind of thing.

- When Frege thought that Wittgenstein was regarding facts as complex objects, he raised a series of simple objections based on the fact that the ways we talk and think of complex objects and their constituent parts do not fit facts at all. For instance, a fundamental feature of the part–whole relationship is that a part of a part of the whole is itself part of the whole: applied to the case of a fact and its constituents that leads to absurdity. Thus if we consider Daphnis and Chloe to be parts of the fact that Daphnis loves Chloe, we seem committed to saying that Daphnis' left foot is part of the fact that Daphnis loves Chloe.

- Facts considered as complex objects seem extremely mysterious entities: it would seem that if we were to specify the 'constituent parts' of the fact that Daphnis loves Chloe, it would be necessary to include not only Daphnis and Chloe, but also the relation of loving – either as a universal, or some particular instance of that relation, and we simply have no understanding of the mode of composition of such disparate entities.

- Connected with the last point, there is a further point: converting the complexity of a fact into the complexity of a complex object falsifies the nature of that complexity. The complexity of facts seems completely different from the complexity of a complex object. We can think of an everyday complex object such as a human being *as* complex, but we are not forced to do so: we give human beings names and talk about them using those names, without giving any thought to their composite nature, and the claims we make about them need contain no indication of the way they are composed of parts, or that they are composed of parts. Whereas, when we specify a fact, such as the fact that Daphnis loves Chloe, we have no alternative but to specify it as complex – we are forced to mention Daphnis and Chloe in the specification. Given any complex object, we can structure it in a number of ways – or, indeed, completely ignore its structure and treat it as simple – whereas a fact, conceived as that to which a proposition is answerable, can *only* be conceived as having a structure that directly reflects the structure of the proposition that represents it.

The trick, then, in understanding Wittgenstein's conception of the world as everything that is the case – the totality of facts to which our propositions are answerable – is not to falsify that conception by conjuring into existence facts as barbarous complex objects.

The world as 'dividing' into facts

So far, we have been using the word 'fact' in a quite general way, so that if someone is in this room, we can talk of the fact that someone is in this room, but to make sense of the rest of the opening paragraphs of the *Tractatus*, we need to give the word 'fact' a more restricted sense. In the broad sense of 'fact', any true proposition will correspond to a fact, but in the narrow sense, facts will always be utterly specific, particular, and such that they can be specified by propositions lacking any logical complexity. The importance of the narrow sense of fact can be brought out as follows: if we consider the (true) proposition that someone is in this room, then what will make it true will not be the bare fact that someone is in this room, but it will always be true in virtue of some particular fact – that Tom is in this room, or that Dick is in this room, or that Harry is in this room, or . . . We will return to this when we look at 4.0312, but we can say in a preliminary way that Wittgenstein's basic idea is that a logically complex, or unspecific, proposition is never barely true – we may say is never true simply in virtue of a logically complex, or unspecific, fact – but is always made true by the underlying particular facts. The spirit of Wittgenstein's position is that strictly speaking there are only particular facts – facts in the narrow sense – and that facts in the broad sense are only called 'facts' in a courtesy or derived sense. He is thinking this through to its logical conclusion and positing a vast kaleidoscope of utterly specific, utterly particular facts, each one consisting in the obtaining or non-obtaining of a specific state of affairs, and the world as consisting in such a kaleidoscope: that *they* constitute 'everything that is the case'.

What is more contentious, and more difficult to justify, is his claim at 1.21, that the world can be broken down into a set of *independent* facts ('every one can be the case or not, while everything else remains the same'). The difficulty with this claim lies in the following consideration: let us consider two different specific shades of colour, *a* and *b*. Then the two claims: that a certain point in space–time is coloured *a*, and that the same point is coloured *b*; both look utterly specific claims, picking out simple states of affairs. But the two claims are clearly incompatible, and the obtaining of one state of affairs rules out the other. Wittgenstein tries to deal with this, but in a highly unsatisfactory manner at 6.3751, yet later came to think that he was clearly mistaken at this point.[6]

What we need to consider are three questions: first, and most importantly: 'Why is Wittgenstein led to say what he says here?' and, more briefly, 'Is what he says here defensible?' and 'What damage does it do to the *Tractatus* if he is wrong on this point?'

To answer the first question we need to consider the phrase he employs in 1.13: 'the facts *in logical space*'. He later seeks to clarify this phrase by saying 'there is an analogy between grammar and geometry'.[7] We can gain an intuitive understanding of what he had in mind if we consider a proposition confronting the vast array of possible obtainings and non-obtainings of particular states of affairs to be carving out a region within those possibilities and saying: 'The truth lies within that region'. 'Grammar' gives to language the necessary degrees of freedom to carve out such a region. But if we take this metaphor of a region seriously, then we think of the world which language confronts as articulated in a way that is analogous to a spatial articulation. If we think then of the states of affairs as located at different points of logical space,[8] the independence of the states of affairs from one another would be the analogue of the idea that there is no logical inference from what is happening at one place in space–time to what is happening at another. A proposition would then build up a picture of reality in a pointillist manner, by indicating which points of logical space were occupied by states of affairs and which were empty.

It is easy to see why Wittgenstein was attracted to this simple model, but if in fact it proved impossible to break the world down into sets of *completely* independent facts, the model would need complicating to allow for that fact. It is not, as is sometimes said, impossible that analysis should break such claims as that a certain point in space–time is coloured *a* and that the same point is coloured *b*, into yet 'simpler' claims, in such a way that one arrived at a set of completely independent states of affairs. But the constructions required to do this begin to look highly artificial. And even if it is possible to break down the set of states of affairs into such an independent set, the question is: 'Was Wittgenstein really justified in insisting that it must be possible?' Assuming it to be possible certainly gives an elegant simplicity to the whole account that Wittgenstein is developing, but that in itself is an insufficient justification for supposing things would necessarily work out that way.

If Wittgenstein is wrong on this point, how much damage does it do to the account he is giving? The answer is: comparatively little; for example, the central claim to which the book builds up – the account of the general form of proposition at proposition 6 – remains intact. The only real point of substance is his claim that 'there is only *logical* necessity' (6.37), when taken together with his truth-functional account of logical truth that we shall be looking at later. A proposition such as: 'if *a* is red, then *a* is not green' would be a necessary truth – a tautology in Wittgenstein's terminology – but it would not be possible to give a purely truth-functional account of that. However, modifying the account of logic to allow for that would greatly complicate the story he is telling, but not undermine its spirit.

Topics for discussion

The most important topics for discussion for this first section all concern the notion of a *fact*, and may be summarized in the following questions:

Is it problematic to take talk of facts seriously, and to regard facts as features of the world?

If we take facts seriously, and think of the world as a world of facts, can we avoid thinking of a fact as a kind of complex object?

Does anything Wittgenstein says in these opening paragraphs commit him, as Frege thought, to thinking of facts as a kind of complex object?

SECTION 2. 'WHAT IS THE CASE, A FACT, IS THE OBTAINING OF STATES OF AFFAIRS'[9]

This section naturally divides into two halves. In the previous section Wittgenstein had seen the world as composed of a network of existing states of affairs. In the first part of this section (2–2.063), he now homes in on the states of affairs themselves, characterizing them as 'combinations of objects'. The crucial part of this discussion, to which we shall devote most attention, is the argument (2.02–2.0201) that these objects must be simple; and that they form 'the substance of the world'. In the second half, Wittgenstein introduces the notion of picturing facts, which prepares the way for one of the main themes of the whole book – that propositions and thoughts are such pictures. Of particular importance for what follows are the following ideas: pictures as models; that a picture is a fact; that it must have something in common with the situation it represents in order to represent it at all; the difference between 'representation' and 'depiction'; and that pictures can be right or wrong, 'true or false'.

In the first section of the *Tractatus*, the world was presented as a vast network of facts, where a fact was characterized as the holding of a state of affairs. In the first half of this section, Wittgenstein amplifies what is meant here by a state of affairs, a state of affairs being initially described in 2.01 as a 'combination of objects'. The point of this characterization will become clearer when we have seen how Wittgenstein's account of propositions as pictures of reality works, but at this stage, we can think of this as a way of explaining the *contingency* of the states of affairs – that a state of affairs may either obtain or not obtain: we think of a range of objects, which may, or may not, combine with one another. If the objects are appropriately combined, then the state of affairs obtains and there is the *fact* that the objects are thus combined; if they are not so combined, then there is not.

It is important here not to prejudge *anything* about the nature of the objects. The argument of the *Tractatus* is *that* there should be such objects, not *what* they should be. We may think of them as those features of reality that can be named by a simple proper name: Wittgenstein is quite clear that we cannot tell *a priori* what the objects actually are. To find out what the objects are, we would have to carry out some form of empirical enquiry – principally we would have to carry out a full analysis of our language. We should not even prejudge such issues as whether the objects are only particulars, or whether they include properties and relations. If we do prejudge such issues, then we will be liable to falsify the account Wittgenstein is building up; the result is likely to be that we make that account look utterly implausible. From time to time in the *Notebooks*, Wittgenstein will for the sake of discussion seem to make assumptions as to the nature of the simple objects – typically, talking as if decomposing a complex object into its simple constituents were a matter of breaking a material object down into smaller material parts, suggesting that an 'object' would be some sort of atomic particle. It is virtually inevitable, when you explore the ideas at stake here that you make use of such illustrations, but they certainly should not be taken as telling us what Wittgenstein thought his simple objects to be and no more should be read into them than is strictly required for the purposes of the illustration. So too, at the end of the first half of this section, I shall present a model to illustrate the way in which all Wittgenstein's demands *might* be satisfied, since that will help us understand the nature of the claims he is making, but this certainly should not be taken to imply that this is the way things would actually work out, or even less that this was what Wittgenstein himself had in mind.

The most we know about the objects of the *Tractatus*, is that they satisfy certain formal demands: (1) That they should be simple (2.02); (2) That the same objects should be common to every world we could possibly imagine (2.022–2.023) and (3) Objects are capable of standing in *immediate* combination with other objects.

It may help in understanding the discussion of the nature of objects that follows to give the spirit of the position Wittgenstein is arguing for. Here for once Wittgenstein's own presentation in the *Philosophical Investigations* of his earlier view is genuinely helpful:

§50 What does it mean to say that we can attribute neither being nor non-being to the elements? – One might say: if everything that we call 'being' and 'non-being' consists in the existence and non-existence of connexions between the elements, it makes no sense to speak of an elements being (non-being); just as when everything that we call 'destruction' lies in the separation of elements, it makes no sense to speak of the destruction of an element.

The existence of a fact consists in objects having been combined in the appropriate way. We are therefore to think of there being a range of objects that form a necessary condition for there being any facts at all. Since these objects are a precondition for there being facts, it cannot simply be a matter of fact that they themselves exist. They rather form the substance of the world: the necessary back-drop for all matters of fact.

Objects as the substance of the world

In 2.02–2.0212 Wittgenstein presents an argument for the simplicity of the 'objects' of the *Tractatus*. This is at one and the same time one of the most elusive in the whole *Tractatus* and one of the most critical arguments in the development of the overall account of the world and the way that language relates to the world. The elliptical way in which Wittgenstein presents his argument here has meant that there is even less agreement as to his intentions than for almost any other passage in the book. It has the form of a *reductio ad absurdum* argument, where the existence of simple objects forming the substance of the world is established from an argument to show that without such simple objects it would be impossible to picture the world at all. Despite the terseness with which Wittgenstein presents his case it is relatively straightforward to fill in the details of his line of thought from 2.0201 through to 2.0211. The central difficulty is the step from 2.0211 to 2.0212.

In what follows I shall present my own interpretation of how that step is supposed to be taken, but at the same time it should be noted that this has been a matter of considerable controversy. The interpretation I shall give here is different from any of those known to me in the literature on the *Tractatus*. One of the more usual lines of interpretation will be indicated as a point for discussion at the end of this section.

Before spelling out the argument, there are a few preliminary points that should be made about it:

- The argument here anticipates ideas that will only be introduced later in the book. While we are still being presented with an account of the world and its contents, the argument depends essentially upon considerations concerning propositions and pic-tures. Here Wittgenstein appears to be inferring facts about the world from the fact that language must be possible. There are other places later on where the inference appears to run the other way (language must be thus and so, otherwise it could not engage with the world). We shall turn to the question of the 'harmony' between the language and the world when we look at 2.16, but that harmony, which legitimizes both forms of inference, is one of the most basic themes, sometimes explicitly but always in the background, throughout the book.

- The chief anticipation of what will come later is clearly the notion of a 'picture of the world'. The point to be noted here is that it is not only the idea that language and thought are a form of picturing reality that is at stake, but a quite particular way of thinking about pictures, the full justification for which will only emerge in Section 3. This way of thinking of pictures is not only critical to the present argument; it is also the point at which it is most vulnerable. In fact a major purpose of the later parts of the *Philosophical Investigations* will be to undermine the way of thinking that led Wittgenstein to think of pictures in the way he does in the *Tractatus*. It is at this point that the most critical engagement between his earlier and later thought is to be found, rather than in the much more superficial criticisms of the *Tractatus* with which he begins the *Investigations*.

- It should be stressed that although this is the passage in which Wittgenstein most explicitly argues for simple objects, there are many different strands in his thinking that lead him to posit their existence. (For instance, as we shall see, they are required for his account of generality and the significance of general propos- itions.) This is one of many places in the *Tractatus* where Wittgenstein is convinced of his key positions not so much because there is a single argument that establishes them as because several different elements in his thinking converge on them. What this means is that Wittgenstein's claim that there are simple objects does not stand or fall with the present argument, and if, as I believe, for all its interest the present argument is subtly flawed, we still have not done with his case for there being such objects.

- In particular, comparison should be made between the present passage and 3.23–3.24. At first sight, some echoes in the ideas presented in the two passages may suggest that we have the same argument for simple objects approached from a somewhat different angle. But in fact there are two completely different argu- ments, and on examination there is considerable tension between the two passages. Although they have the same conclusion (the need for simple objects) the present passage derives that conclusion from the need for the world to 'have substance', the later passage from the 'demand that sense be determinate'. As a result, they imply a quite different conception of the relation between a complex and its constituents, and a quite different conception of the analysis of propositions. The second passage stems from a later stage in Wittgenstein's thinking from the first, and, in fact, if we were to reconcile the two texts, the first passage would need modification to take account of what is said in the second. (In particular, 2.0201 would need to be altered.) But at this stage, we will tease out the argument purely in its own terms.

The argument takes its starting point at 2.0201 in what Wittgenstein at one point called 'the theory of the complex':

> The theory of the complex is expressed in such propositions as: 'If a proposition is true then Something exists'; there seems to be a difference between the fact expressed by the proposition: a stands in the relation R to b, and the complex *a in the relation R to b*, which is just that which exists if that proposition is true. It seems as if we could *designate* this Something, and what's more with a real 'complex sign'.[10]

The idea here seems to be that if a proposition is true, there is something in the world in virtue of which it is true, and hence a complex entity that makes the proposition true. So that if the cat is sitting on the mat, there exists the *cat-is-sitting-on-the-mat* complex. Wittgenstein differentiates this entity from the fact that the cat is sitting on the mat – which is not an object at all, either simple or complex. He adopts the convention of denoting the complex corresponding to the true proposition 'aRb' by the sign '[aRb]', and we may say that '[aRb] exists' is equivalent to 'aRb'. The constituents of such a complex will be the objects referred to in the proposition. (It is, however, worth asking whether the properties and relations mentioned in the proposition are also to be counted as its constituents. Are the constituents of [*The-cat-is-sitting-on-the-mat*], the cat and the mat, or, the cat, the mat and the relation between them? If we say that only the cat and the mat are constituents, then it seems impossible, e.g., to differentiate the [*Tom-is-fatter-than-Dick*] complex from the [*Tom-is-taller-than-Dick*] complex, since both seem to collapse into an amalgam of Tom and Dick. If, however, we say that we should also count the relation between them as a further constituent, then they become somewhat mysterious entities, quite unlike what we would ordinarily consider to be complex objects.)[11]

As the discussion progresses, Wittgenstein seems to assume, without comment, that everyday objects such as watches, people and books are complexes in the sense just explained. But although he does not comment on this, it is a step that needs justifying: it is not justified simply by the obvious fact that these objects are significantly composed of parts, and hence have constituents, since that would simply be a play on the word 'constituent'. What is required is to show that they have constituents in the sense outlined in the preceding paragraph. If that is to be justified, it would be by the consideration, which Wittgenstein certainly requires for his argument, that such objects are *contingent* entities: this watch might not have existed, and we can readily imagine how things would have been if it had not existed. That implies that there is a true proposition to the effect that this watch does indeed exist. In accordance with the preceding paragraph, that proposition will have a complex associated with it, which, like the watch itself, will exist if and only if that proposition is true. We therefore take the step of identifying the watch with that complex, and the entities mentioned in the proposition as the constituents of the watch. (It should be noted that if we follow this train of thought, there is no reason to suppose that the 'constituents' of the watch have to be the material parts of which it is composed.)

Against this background, it is easy to interpret 2.0201. Let us suppose that we are concerned with a proposition about a particular teapot, such as: 'The teapot weighs five ounces', and we view the teapot as a complex whose constituents are the pot and the lid, so that the teapot exists if and only if the lid is in the pot.[12] Then we may rewrite the proposition in the form: '[*The-lid-is-in-the-pot*] complex weighs five ounces', which we then analyse in the form: 'The lid is in the pot, and the sum of the weights of the pot and the lid is five ounces'. It is the first clause of this proposition that Wittgenstein has in mind when he talks of 'the propositions that describe the complex completely'. If, then, the pot and the lid are themselves complexes, we may repeat the process of analysis, arriving at a yet more complicated proposition. Such repetitions may either go on for ever, at each stage uncovering further complex entities, or they eventually terminate. But the only way they can terminate is if we reach a stage at which a proposition about a complex is analysed into propositions about constituents that are not themselves complexes: i.e. are simple objects of which it makes no sense to say that they might not exist.

So the questions that arise are: 'Why does it matter if the process of analysis just outlined would never terminate?' and, even more basically, 'What is the point of engaging in such analysis at all?' Even if we grant that 'The teapot weighs five ounces' is equivalent to 'The lid is in the pot, and the sum of the weights of the pot and the lid is five ounces', why analyse the former as the latter and not simply accept it as it is? Wittgenstein's initial answer is to be found in 2.0211: if we could not complete the process of analysis in the way that has just been outlined, then 'whether one proposition made sense would depend upon the truth of another'. His thought here can be spelled out as follows: suppose we consider a proposition that mentions a contingent entity, e. g. a proposition containing the proper name of a human being, such as 'Socrates was wise'. On an everyday understanding of this proposition, Socrates is named in this proposition, and a property is ascribed to him, so that the proposition is true or false according as Socrates was, or was not wise. But that understanding presupposes the existence of Socrates and the proposition is only true or false (which for Wittgenstein would be for the proposition to have a sense) on the assumption that there was indeed such a person as Socrates. But even if we know it to be true, 'There was such a person as Socrates' is a significant proposition, and our original proposition would only make sense if this other proposition was true.

The question now is: 'Why does that matter?' After all, we seem to have no trouble in naming the people that happen to be around us, and in talking about them. The fact that, if they had not existed, we would not have been able to give the sense that we do to the propositions that we formulate about them, does not create any obvious difficulty for our use of language. Wittgenstein's answer at this point is 2.0212: 'It would then be impossible to form a picture of the world (true or false)'. Here Wittgenstein's thought is outrageously compressed, particularly since he here introduces without warning the idea of picturing into the discussion, although it is only later on in the text that he will present picturing as fundamental to his whole account of language and thought. It is at that later stage that the quite particular way of thinking of pictures which is required by his account will be argued for. At this stage I shall simply sketch those features of his account that are necessary to understand the present argument.

- Included in the picture is its representational relation to reality (2.1513). Wittgenstein is including as a component of the picture the fact that the picture depicts what it does.
- The second requirement is counterintuitive, but, I believe, necessary for an understanding both of the present argument, and also of his conception of thought that we shall examine at the beginning of the next section. We will look at why Wittgenstein is laying this requirement on the concept of *picture* at the beginning of Section 3, and for present purposes simply explain it sufficiently to show how it underpins the present argument. Wittgenstein is insisting on a conception of pictures according to which it is an *intrinsic* property of a picture that it *is* a picture, and *what* it is a picture of. It must be possible to tell that a picture is a picture, and what it is a picture of, from the picture itself without reference to anything outside.

With this in mind, consider a picture – a picture of Napoleon leading his army to Moscow, say – or the proposition: 'In 1812, Napoleon led his army to Moscow', since although he has not yet argued for this, Wittgenstein is here presupposing that propositions are special cases of pictures. It is a contingent matter of fact that there was such a person as Napoleon. Therefore if we make the possibility of there being such a picture of Napoleon leading his army to Moscow depend upon the existence of Napoleon, the picture's being a picture depends upon something extrinsic to the picture, whose existence cannot be inferred simply by studying the picture itself. (NB here and throughout the *Tractatus* Wittgenstein is only concerned with pictures of reality and not with pictures depicting fictions.) Hence if we insist upon its being an *intrinsic* property of a picture that it pictures what it does, we must explain the possibility of picturing Napoleon in a way that does not depend on his having existed. We therefore break down the picture (proposition) about Napoleon into simpler pictures (propositions) in the way sketched above, where the simple constituents represented in those pictures are such that we have an *a priori* guarantee of their existence. Since the existence of these constituents is thus guaranteed, we do not need to refer outside the picture itself to know if there is anything that it is a picture of.

Objects as simple

When Wittgenstein characterizes objects as simple, one is initially likely to think of them as tiny, like the atoms of ancient Greek Philosophy or Newton's infinitesimals. But that encourages the wrong way of thinking about them. Later at 3.24 he will argue directly for the simplicity of the objects. In the present context, however, Wittgenstein infers the simplicity of the objects from their 'forming the substance of the world' – we may say as shorthand their 'necessary existence'. It is that which provides the clue to the correct way of understanding what is meant by 'simplicity' here. The objects are simple, in the sense that they are not complexes, in the sense of 'the theory of the complex' sketched above: if they were complexes, their existence would be contingent and to be analysed in the way outlined in the argument we have been looking at.

The 'necessary' existence of the objects

It is natural to think of Wittgenstein's objects as 'existing necessarily', but that way of putting matters falsifies Wittgenstein's intentions. It is better to say that they *unquestionably* exist, meaning thereby that we can attach no sense to the question whether or not they exist. The conception that we have arrived at is that there is a range of objects that constitute a necessary precondition for language (for 'forming a picture of the world'). Since they are a necessary precondition for language, to imagine a world very different from the actual one cannot be to imagine a world in which these objects do not exist (2.022): it is to imagine a world in which precisely *these* objects are recombined in a different way from the way they are in reality. Also, since they are a necessary precondition for language, we cannot ask *within* language whether or not they exist. Here we have the first hint of an idea that is central to the whole of the *Tractatus*: we cannot ask whether or not the objects exist, and we cannot *say* that the objects exist (necessarily), but what leads us to want to say that the objects exist necessarily is something that is *shown* by the way that our language functions.

States of affairs as objects in immediate combination

2.03 In a state of affairs objects hang one in another, like the links of a chain.

I shall only comment briefly on this passage, although it is a crucial element in Wittgenstein's conception of a state of affairs. It is difficult to put his point non-metaphorically without the use of an example. The basic idea, however, is that the objects combine *immediately* with one another, without the need of any connecting link. What this means is that one can specify a state of affairs simply by specifying what objects are combined with each other, without in addition having to specify how those objects are related: this will perhaps become clearer when we have looked at an example of the way this might work out.

Objects as the form of the world

In 2.023, Wittgenstein talks of the objects as constituting the 'fixed form' of the world. This certainly sounds odd if we think that the objects that Wittgenstein is talking about are material particles or the like. We can, however, make sense of this way of talking if we consider the idea that we introduced in Section 1 of the states of affairs as located at different points of logical space. Wittgenstein himself claimed not to know what instances of the objects actually were, but among the examples that he tended to recur to as possibilities were spatial entities such as 'a point in visual space'.[13] Consider also a passage such as the following from the *Notebooks*:

We might construe two co-ordinates a_p and b_p as a proposition stating that the material point P is to be found at the location (ab). For such an assertion to be possible there the co-ordinates a and b must actually define a location. For an assertion to be possible, the logical co-ordinates must actually define a logical location![14]

We can follow up such suggestions by constructing an illustration of the kind of way in which the ideas we have been looking at so far in this section might work out. (Of course, it must be stressed that this is no more than an illustration: the actual structure of logical space might be very different from this – it would almost certainly be *far* more complicated than this simple model would suggest.) Let us assume that we live in a Euclidean three-dimensional space, throughout which are scattered Newtonian particles of matter, so that the world would be completely specified by, say, where there were and where there were not particles of matter. We may then think of a state of affairs as the existence of a Newtonian point mass at a certain position in space–time: we may specify such a position by Cartesian co-ordinates – (x, y, z, t). If we take the objects of the *Tractatus*, then, to be the planes of space and time instants, we may construe a state of affairs as consisting in the fact that three planes at a certain time intersect at a point mass. The 'necessity' of the objects in this model consists in the fact that we cannot imagine what it would be for space to exist without some particular plane of space existing. Every state of affairs may be thought of as a combination of objects. The states of affairs will be logically independent of one another and the world will be completely specified by specifying precisely which states of affairs exist.

Of course, the actual structure of logical space would be much more complicated than that envisaged in this simple model, but I suggest that it would be simply a far more complicated version of this model that would be required if we were to satisfy all the requirements Wittgenstein is arguing for in this section.

Pictures

2.1 We make ourselves pictures of the facts.

In the second half of this section, beginning at 2.1, Wittgenstein introduces the idea of picturing. We will treat this part of the section more briefly than the first half, since the themes introduced here will recur later in greater detail. The idea of picturing will have central significance for all that follows, and will dominate the next two sections that are concerned with thoughts and propositions, precisely because the basic claim that Wittgenstein is arguing for is that thoughts and propositions are pictures of reality. In this section, he is simply outlining some of his key theses concerning pictures that will be important in what is to follow.

Pictures as models
At 2.12, pictures are explained as models. The notion of a model that Wittgenstein is employing is a very simple notion: we model the way

one set of objects is arranged, by letting another set of objects stand in for the first set, with each object in the first set having a corresponding object in the second. The second set of objects are arranged in a specific way to represent that the first set of objects are arranged in a corresponding way (2.15).[15] We can think of this as the reproduction of a situation in another medium. It is easy to see how such a notion of modelling can be applied to the simple case of the states of affairs that we considered at the beginning of this section. There we have a set of objects combined in a specific way, and we can readily produce another set of objects that are to be combined in a corresponding way. Wittgenstein, however, is putting forward here and elsewhere (4.01) the more radical and initially puzzling claim that *all* pictures are models in this sense, including e.g. someone's portrait, or, eventually, the propositions that we use in everyday speech – upon analysis these too turn out to be models. Some commentators have wanted to restrict the application of the 'Picture Theory of the Proposition' to the simple case of propositions that represent states of affairs (such propositions Wittgenstein will call 'elementary propositions'), so that strictly speaking Wittgenstein should not say that *all* pictures and propositions are models, but that elementary propositions are such models, and that we can use truth-functions (see proposition 5 below) to build complex propositions and pictures out of such elementary pictures. But that is clearly not Wittgenstein's intention: at every point his claims about models and pictures are made with complete generality. So the problem that we need to consider is: 'How does Wittgenstein think that his conception of pictures as models can have any application to highly complex cases of pictures and propositions?' This is the question that we shall examine in Section 4, at 4.0312 and the paragraphs following.

Pictures as facts

At 2.141 the next crucial feature of Wittgenstein's conception of pictures is introduced: the idea of a picture as a fact. It is natural initially to think of a picture as a complex object – a rectangle of canvas on which has been painted a scatter of oil paint, say. However, when we think about the picture, conceived as such a complex object, it is obvious that we may differentiate those features of the object that have representative significance and those which do not. Thus there is nothing in reality corresponding to the fact that oil paint has been used in the production of the picture; the different colours of the patches of paint, however, may well represent that the objects in the situation represented are coloured in a corresponding way. So too the spatial distribution of the patches of paint may represent a corresponding spatial arrangement of the objects represented. Wittgenstein is equating the picture not with the complex physical object, but with the sum total of those facts that have representative significance: the fact that the elements in the picture are related to one another in a specific way representing a situation in which objects are related to one another in a corresponding way (2.15).

We may think of this as follows: Wittgenstein is conceiving a picture as the reproduction of a situation in another medium. Consider the simplest kind of modelling: let us say, the representation of a water molecule, using ping-pong balls for the hydrogen and oxygen atoms. Here we could have two pink ping-pong balls wired up to a single blue ping-pong ball. There is then nothing pink or blue in the situation represented, but the fact that the balls are arranged in a specific way reproduces the corresponding arrangement of the atoms. We shall return to the idea that a picture is a fact in the next section at 3.14.

Pictures as having something in common with what they depict
One theme that dominates the whole of the *Tractatus* is the idea that if a picture is to depict a situation, rightly or wrongly, it must have something in common with that situation in order that it should be able to depict it at all. This theme also introduces one of the key ideas of the book: that a picture does not depict what it must have in common with the situation it depicts, but *shows* it (2.172) and that what can be shown cannot be said. This will be discussed further at 4.121. In the present context, I shall simply illustrate the basic idea.

Suppose that we wish to represent the spatial relationships between a set of objects – a soldier may use various bits of cruet to illustrate the relative positions of the different forces in a battle, with the salt standing for the enemy artillery, the pepper his side's tanks and so on. Then the representation will represent a specific spatial relation between the opposing forces by setting up a specific spatial relation between the different pots set out on the tablecloth. The soldier may, or may not, represent the spatial relation correctly. But there is one thing that he must do if he is to represent the battle at all: he must put the different bits of cruet in a spatial relation with one another. He represents a spatial relationship by a spatial relationship: this is so, even if he represents the particular spatial relationship of the forces incorrectly. His representation does not *say* that the forces in the battle are spatially related; what it does *say* is what the particular spatial relationships they stand in are. That they are spatially related is something that is presupposed by the technique of representation: unless you understand that here spatial relations represent spatial relations, you will not be able to understand the representation as a representation at all. The representation *shows* but does not say that the forces on the ground are spatially related.

Now, of course, we may adopt highly artificial techniques of representation, so that e.g. spatial relationships are not portrayed by spatial relationships but by some other relationship between elements. We may represent the profits and losses of a company by a line on a graph, the percentages of people voting for particular political parties by pie charts, and Wittgenstein himself will talk of the musical score or the groove in the gramophone record as pictures of the symphony (4.014). The more artificial the technique of representation, the more attenuated the idea of the picture having something in common with what it depicts seems to become: there seems to be little in common between the groove on the gramophone record and the symphony. But no matter how attenuated, Wittgenstein is claiming that there is a minimal *logical* form that must be shared by the picture and what it depicts: they must possess the same 'logical multiplicity'. We will return to this contention in section 4 at 4.04.

Representation and depiction
The main point to make here is a terminological one, although one which has important implications. Wittgenstein is distinguishing two different concepts for which he uses the words '*Abbildung*' and '*Darstellung*', both of which are in normal German translatable as 'representation', but in Wittgenstein's use are to be differentiated. I follow both the translations of the *Tractatus* in rendering '*Abbildung*' as 'depiction' and '*Darstellung*' as 'representation'.[16] The distinction can be brought out by noting that Wittgenstein always uses these terms with different objects: a picture depicts *reality*, but represents a *situation*. We can illustrate the difference as follows. Suppose we have a picture showing Socrates to be clean-shaven, where in reality Socrates may or may not be so. (We may suppose him in fact to have been bearded.) Such a picture *represents* the situation of Socrates

being clean-shaven, but is a depiction of the reality with which the picture is to be compared: the actual state of Socrates, his bearded state. What the picture *represents* is internal to the picture and may be read off the picture itself. What it *depicts* is something in the world with which the picture is to be compared. It is because we may think of a picture both as a representation of a situation and as a depiction of reality that the picture can *misrepresent* (2.21): the picture we are considering misrepresents Socrates by representing him as being in a state that is different from his actual state.

The importance of being able to regard a picture both as a representation and as a depiction is that this provides a preliminary indication of the way in which seeing propositions as pictures helps to explain the most basic feature of propositions – their being true-or-false. A proposition is true if what it represents agrees with what it depicts, false if it disagrees.

Topics for discussion

My interpretation of the argument at 2.02–2.0212 is not a standard one. It is far more usual to find interpretations that take Wittgenstein to be assuming a strong form of *bivalence*: a proposition only makes sense if it is impossible to specify a possible world in which it is neither true nor false. How convincing do you find my interpretation? Is there an alternative you would prefer?

Test out whether the different claims that Wittgenstein makes in this section would be satisfied in the model I suggested when commenting on 2.023. How far does such a model help to make sense of those claims?

SECTION 3. 'A LOGICAL PICTURE OF THE FACTS IS A THOUGHT'

'A logical picture of the facts is a thought.' Pictures and propositional signs as facts. Simples and Complexes. Determinacy of sense. The 'Context Principle'; expressions as propositional variables; sign and symbol.

The idea of picturing and of propositions as pictures is important to Wittgenstein's thought in two different ways. The first, which concerns us here, is that Wittgenstein is to argue that an analysis of what is involved in *thinking* requires us to conceive of a proposition as a picture. The second, which forms the subject of the opening paragraphs of the next section, is that he will there argue that only if propositions are pictures can we make sense of their being true or false. Although these two ideas will have dovetailed into each other in Wittgenstein's mind, they are separate arguments and it is important to consider them as such. This is especially true if, as I believe, at least in the way that Wittgenstein develops it, the present conception of propositions as pictures is directly bound up with a particular way of thinking about issues in the philosophy of mind that is subjected to a sustained critique in the *Philosophical Investigations*. It would take us too far afield to look at that critique in the present book. But that critique would leave the arguments of the next section for regarding propositions as pictures completely untouched. There Wittgenstein will argue that it is only if we think of propositions as pictures that we can explain how it is possible that they should be true or false. *That* argument is not vulnerable to an attack on the conception of mental phenomena that he seems to be adopting here.

The basic idea in this section is quite simple: I must *know* what I am thinking, and therefore if I am thinking about a particular situation then there must be in my mind something that is essentially connected with that situation. Obviously the situation itself is not in my mind; therefore there must be some surrogate for that situation from which it is possible to reconstruct the actual situation. Only a model or picture of the situation would fit the bill of being such a surrogate. What is more, that surrogate must be *internally* related to the situation being thought about, so that if that surrogate occurs in my mind there is an *a priori* guarantee that it is precisely that situation that is being thought about.[17] If there were only some *external* relation, such as a causal relation, between what was in my mind and the situation, then what was in my mind would carry with it no guarantee as to what I was thinking. This is what Wittgenstein has in mind when he says at 2.1511 that a picture 'reaches up to reality'. If this were not so, I would not be able to think about reality at all and it would never be correct to say that I am thinking about Napoleon, say, but only that I have an idea that as a matter of fact is in some way causally connected with Napoleon.

But this leads on to the idea that I claimed was crucial to the argument at 2.02–2.0212. Not only must the picture be essentially connected to the situation that it is a picture of, but it must be an intrinsic property of the picture that it is a picture, and that it is a picture of that situation: the picture must contain within itself the possibility of the situation that it represents (2.203). It is this further demand that underpins the argument for simple objects in Section 2 as I interpreted it. If thinking is a matter of having a picture of the situation being thought about and this demand were not satisfied, then I would be in doubt whether I was thinking, or what I was thinking. The thought that lies behind the whole of Wittgenstein's discussion is that I must be able to *know* what I mean, and what I am thinking.

Note also, he does not simply say in proposition 3 that thinking *involves the use of* pictures, but actually equates the thought with the picture: if the picture occurs to me in the appropriate way, then I am *ipso facto* thinking that the situation represented by the picture obtains. Thinking here is not seen as forming a picture of the situation that *p* is the case, and also saying to oneself 'That's how things are': to form the picture in the appropriate way is *already* to think that *p*. (Otherwise one would be involved in an unwanted infinite regress.)

Propositional signs as facts

At 3.14, Wittgenstein now applies the claim of 2.141 to the specific case of propositional signs. As with all pictures, they are not to be viewed as complex objects, but as facts. There are two passages here that merit particular attention – 3.141–3.142 and 3.1432.

Although Wittgenstein's treatment is extremely brief, in 3.141–3.142 he highlights one of the most important reasons for regarding propositions as facts. So regarding them provides an elegant solution to a problem that had troubled Frege. Any account of propositions had to reconcile two opposing ideas that we have about propositions: that a proposition is essentially complex and that it is equally essential to a proposition that the words in the proposition should combine to express a *single* thought. What constitutes the *unity* of a proposition? How does a propositional sign differ from a list of words? I do exactly the same thing when I write down the words 'John', 'loves' and 'Mary' one after the other as a list of words as when I write down the propositional sign 'John loves Mary'. In both cases I produce a complex object whose parts are 'John', 'loves' and 'Mary', but in the latter case I have written down something that expresses a *single* thought. For Wittgenstein, these questions are answered once you see the propositional sign, not as the complex object that I have indeed produced, but as the *fact* that the words 'John', 'loves' and 'Mary' are arranged in a specific way. To apprehend the propositional sign as a propositional sign is precisely to pick out that single fact.

The next two paragraphs – 3.143 and 3.1431 – are far from helpful. In fact, although one can see what led Wittgenstein to say what he says here, the thought is a bad one. There is *no* mode of expression that would obviate the potential confusion between viewing the propositional sign as a complex object and viewing it as a fact. There is no good reason to suppose that if we used bits of furniture to form propositional signs, people might not take the propositional sign to be the complex object whose parts were those bits of furniture.

Proposition 3.1432 is a spelling out of what it amounts to to regard the propositional sign as a fact. When we consider the propositional sign 'John loves Mary', we are not to say that the sentence 'John loves Mary', viewed as a complex object, says that John stands in the relation of loving to Mary, but the fact *that* the names 'John' and 'Mary' flank the word 'loves' says *that* John loves Mary.

In this way, in a proposition we have a fact modelling a situation, a recreation of that situation in another medium. We may think of this by analogy with a police reconstruction of a crime. Just as in the police reconstruction, a policewoman will stand in for the victim, a policeman for the criminal and the way that they are related will show the way that the crime is supposed to have happened, so on this account of the propositional sign, 'John' stands in for John, 'Mary' for Mary and the specific relation we set up between those names will show the way that John is claimed to be related to Mary.

What this account does is highlight the rôle of *names* in language, and explain how they are supposed to function. Names are the elements in the propositional sign that stand in for objects, so that Wittgenstein can even say 'the name means the object' (3.203), and therefore in the 3.2s he turns to the question of the nature of names.

The principal point that he makes about names is that they are *simple* signs (3.202). By this he means that they are *essentially* simple: a sign could be typographically simple, but actually function as an abbreviation for a complex phrase. Names, however, cannot be regarded as abbreviations for anything more complex (3.26). To say that a name is simple means that you give a *complete* characterization of the meaning of a name, its rôle in language, by saying that it stands in for an object in propositions and its meaning is simply the fact that it stands in for the object it does.

This leads on to the question: 'Which then are the *genuine* names of the language?' We already saw at 2.0201 that Wittgenstein is not taking for granted that the everyday names we give to complex objects do function as names by his criterion. They will typically be abbreviations for some complex phrase. Wittgenstein is now to argue that the only genuinely simple signs – the *names* of the language – will be names of objects that are themselves simple.

In 3.23 Wittgenstein claims that the 'demand for determinacy of sense' requires there to be simple signs, and presents his argument for that claim in 3.24, the key paragraph being the third:

> That a propositional element signifies a complex can be seen from an indeterminacy in the propositions in which it occurs. We *know* that such a proposition leaves something undetermined. (Indeed, the quantifier notation *contains* a prototype.)

This is a crucial passage for an understanding of Wittgenstein's conception of the analysis of propositions and for his claim that there must be simple objects. Because of that, and because the passage is highly obscure, I will devote a lot of space to it. At first sight, this passage seems to contain some echoes of the argument for simple objects that we looked at in 2.02–2.0211. In particular, the opening sentences of 3.24 can appear to be a reformulation of 2.0201. But in fact we have not only two quite different arguments, but there are deep tensions between the two passages.

In the first place, the premises of the two arguments are completely different. The earlier passage took as its starting point a particular way of thinking of pictures, taken together with the idea that such pictures must be possible. The present passage does not in any way depend upon such a way of thinking of pictures, or even on the idea that propositions are pictures. Instead, it introduces a new idea, not present in the earlier discussion: the idea that 'sense must be determinate'. However, not only are the two arguments different, so too are the conclusions of the arguments. Both argue for the possibility of analysing any proposition that mentions a complex into a set of propositions about simple objects, but fully worked out they would lead to significantly different analyses of a proposition mentioning a complex. In fact, if you look through the background discussions in the *Notebooks*, you will discover that 2.02–2.0211 and 3.23–3.24 stem from two different stages in Wittgenstein's thinking, and that to reconcile the two passages, we would need to modify what Wittgenstein says in the earlier passage so as to accommodate the ideas of the later passage, which we must now examine in detail. The compression of the text here is extreme, so that it is almost inevitable that one consults the *Notebooks*, and one of the best ways to unpack the argument of 3.23–3.24 is to track through the progression of Wittgenstein's thought in the *Notebooks*.[18]

But first we must decide what Wittgenstein means here by 'determinate' (*bestimmt*), and as a result understand why there should be a 'demand that sense be determinate'. It is possible to interpret this word in two quite distinct ways: we may interpret 'indeterminate' either as meaning 'vague' or as meaning 'unspecific'. We may explain the difference as follows: we shall call a proposition 'vague' if there is no clear answer to the question whether it is true or false; we shall call it 'unspecific' if there is a wide range of ways in which it could be true. We can illustrate the difference by considering the following:

Some of Schubert's late works are typical of early romanticism.

This proposition can be seen as both vague and unspecific: it is vague, because the lack of clear-cut criteria as to what is and what is not romanticism make it impossible to assign it a definite truth value; it is unspecific, because it does not specify *which* of Schubert's works are in question. We can see that these are two different ideas by changing the example. If we say:

Schubert's *Winterreise* is typical of early romanticism.

Then the proposition is more specific, but equally vague.

In the entries in the *Notebooks*, there are both remarks that are concerned with the problem of giving an account of a vague language and remarks that are concerned with the problem of giving an account of an unspecific language. Many remarks could be equally concerned with either. It could even be that the two notions were not clearly distinguished in Wittgenstein's mind. However, when we consider the immediate context in the *Notebooks* in which the original version of 3.24 appears,[19] it seems clear that we should take '*Unbestimmtheit*' here to mean 'lack of specificity' and not 'vagueness' when we interpret 3.24 itself: it is in any case impossible to see how the argument of 3.24 is to be spelled out if we take '*Unbestimmtheit*' as vagueness.

With this understanding of what is meant by determinacy, what is the force of 'the *demand* that sense be determinate'? One of the clearest answers to that question can be found in the following passage from the *Notebooks*:

> It does not go against our feeling, that *we* cannot analyse PROPO-SITIONS so far as to mention the elements by name; no, we feel that the WORLD must consist of elements. And it appears as if that were identical with the proposition that the world must be what it is, it must be definite. Or in other words, what vacillate are our determinations, not the world. It looks as if to deny things were as much as to say that the world can, as it were, be indeterminate in some such sense as that in which our knowledge is uncertain and indeterminate.
> The world has a fixed structure.[20]

Taking 'determinacy' to mean 'specificity', the basic idea is that lack of specificity is a feature of our language, not of the world. The propositions that we utter are all more or less specific, but it makes no sense to talk of the situations in the world that actually make them true or false as lacking specificity. So that if I say: 'Tom owed some money' then that is in various ways unspecific – it 'leaves possibilities open' as Wittgenstein repeatedly says in the *Notebooks*, but if true, it will always be made true by some absolutely specific situation. Thus the proposition doesn't say to whom Tom owes money, or how much, or . . ., but it cannot be made true by Tom-owing-money-to-someone without there being some specific nameable individual to whom the money is owed. The sense of the unspecific proposition then is such that it picks out a *range* of specific situations, any one of which would make it true if it actually obtained. What is more, anyone who understands the proposition would be able to recognize any one of those specific situations as one that would make what was said true, and as Wittgenstein puts it,[21] this is 'settled in advance'. If a certain situation makes what I say true, then that proposition must be such that it had a sense which specifies that situation as one of the situations that would make it true prior to the actual occurrence of that situation.

For these reasons, it must be possible to spell out the sense of a proposition in such a way as to show explicitly the range of specific situations that would make it true – in fact to represent it as a vast disjunction of utterly specific claims, each of which picks out a specific situation that, were it to occur, would make the proposition true. Now, to make Wittgenstein's argument easier to follow I shall introduce a notion that he doesn't actually introduce explicitly until 4.21 – that of an 'elementary proposition'. We may think of an elementary proposition as a proposition that is void of any logical complexity and that represents a single utterly specific state of affairs. Such a proposition will model that state of affairs in the most straightforward way imaginable: it will be an arrangement of names, modelling a corresponding arrangement of objects in the state of affairs. To show the way in which 'sense is determinate' – that is to say, the way in which our everyday unspecific claims are nevertheless always made true or false by the utterly specific concrete detail of what actually happens in the world – we now represent the sense of a given proposition by showing which combinations of truth and falsity of the elementary propositions make it true, and which false. We will call a representation that exhibits a proposition in such a way a 'complete analysis' of the proposition, since it shows in detail how the proposition is made true or false by the concrete detail of the world – shows how the proposition 'reaches right up to reality' (2.1511). Such a complete analysis would make clear the *internal* relation between the proposition and the specific situations which, were they to obtain, would make the proposition true.

The 'genuine' names of the language will then be the names that can occur in elementary propositions (4.23). So the question to be addressed is: 'Could these names include names of complex objects?' or 'Could a name of a complex object occur in an elementary proposition?' In the *Notebooks* we can see Wittgenstein as wrestling with this question, torn between three conflicting positions. (1) In the first instance, we take at face value our everyday practice of naming people, animals and the other complex objects that we see around us. After all, we unthinkingly and naturally *do* name such things, and we seem to run into no problems in doing so. (2) Propositions about complex objects are to be analysed into propositions about the constituents of those complexes, along the lines we looked at when we interpreted 2.02–2.0211. (3) The third position, which may be regarded as an objection to the second of these three positions, is the one with which the argument of 3.24 is concerned.

In the *Notebooks*, he explores such propositions as: 'The watch is on the table' and the possibility of breaking them down into propositions about the constituents of the watch which, for the purposes of discussion, he takes to be the bits of glass and metal – the various hands, springs, wheels etc. Initially he does this along the lines indicated at 2.021. A proposition about the watch will then be tantamount to a proposition about how those bits have been arranged in such a way that the watch exists, together with further propositions about those bits that are tantamount to saying that the resulting watch is indeed on the table. This exploration leads to the apparently extravagant claim:

> When I say this watch is shiny, and what I mean by this watch alters its composition in the smallest particular, then this means not merely that the sense of the sentence alters in its content, but also *what I am saying about this watch* straightway alters its sense. The whole form of the proposition alters.[22]

Extravagant though that is, the thought is clear: if a proposition about a watch is to be analysed down into propositions about its constituents, then if one of those constituents were missing – a tiny wheel that had no obvious effect on the smooth running of the watch, say – then a whole series of clauses in the analysis, namely, those that mention the wheel, would have to be omitted, producing a proposition with a completely different logical form. It is Wittgenstein's rejoinder to this line of thought that will form the argument of 3.24:

> If, *e.g.*, I say that this watch is not in the drawer, there is absolutely no need for it to FOLLOW LOGICALLY that a wheel which is in the watch is not in the drawer, and hence could not have meant by 'this watch' the complex in which the wheel occurs.[23]

When someone makes a claim about a watch, they will have a limited knowledge of its actual composition – in most cases, an extremely limited knowledge. This means that it will be impossible to analyse what they mean in terms of the *actual* composition of the watch. What they will know is that *some* set of bits of glass, wheels, etc., have been assembled *somehow* so as to produce the watch, introducing a high degree of indeterminacy (lack of specificity) into the analysis of what they mean:

> For if I am talking about, *e.g.*, this watch and mean something complex by that and nothing depends upon the way it is

compounded, then a generalization will make its appearance the proposition.[24]

What this means is that the propositions that we ordinarily utter in which names of everyday complex objects appear turn out on analysis to be highly unspecific: the claims we make about a watch will typically be compatible with a wide variety of detailed ways in which the watch has been assembled: we will have to employ generalizations in our account if we wish to spell out in detail what would make what we say true.[25]

If, then, on the one hand, elementary propositions are utterly specific, and on the other hand propositions containing names of complex objects always turn out upon examination to be highly unspecific, no elementary proposition can contain the name of a complex. If, however, elementary propositions are composed of names, then these names can only be names of objects that are simple. Hence, if elementary propositions are to be possible, there must *be* simple objects.

It may help to understand this argument, by comparing this case with another case where few people will be tempted to regard a sign as a name. Consider the word 'inflation'. If we take the proposition 'Inflation rose last month', it looks highly unattractive to say that in this proposition 'inflation' names an object, and that the proposition says of this object that it has the property of having risen last month. If we were to explain the sense of this proposition to someone, we would instead talk about the vast network of concrete financial transactions – Mrs Smith buying a house, Mr Jones buying a loaf of bread, etc. – that occurred during the relevant period, and what must be the case for those financial transactions to make it true that 'Inflation rose last month'. The proposition 'Inflation rose last month' could not be *barely* true, without there being a range of specific financial transactions and there being certain things that were true of those transactions. Anyone understanding the proposition would in principle be able to work out whether the proposition was true, if they were given full detailed knowledge of the buyings and sellings that actually occurred. We could therefore in principle break the proposition 'Inflation rose last month' into a vastly complex statement about the financial transactions that actually occurred.

However, although the claim that 'Inflation rose last month' can only be made true by the actual financial transactions being of a certain sort, it does not tell you *which* financial transactions in fact occurred. It is compatible with a vast range of possible sets of financial transactions having occurred. If then we were to spell out the sense of the proposition in terms of such financial transactions, we would have to represent it as a vast disjunction of possibilities. In this way, the proposition would be radically unspecific, but would always be made true or false by buyings and sellings that were specific. Thus we can never achieve full specificity by using propositions containing the word 'inflation' and if we want to know what specifically such a proposition amounts to, we always have to break such a proposition down into propositions about the financial transactions that actually occur in the world. This fact gives strong backing to our intuition that it is misguided to regard the word 'inflation' as a name. We can regard the argument of 3.24 as an argument to show that the everyday names that we use for complex objects are in the same boat as the word 'inflation'.

Primitive and defined signs
Wittgenstein now contrasts primitive and defined signs (3.26–3.261), with names as the paradigm case of primitive signs. Defined signs are signs whose meanings can be explained in terms of other signs, whereas primitive signs are the signs used in those explanations, but which cannot themselves be so defined. This leads to the questions that follow: 'How do we tell whether a sign is primitive or defined?' and 'How could we explain the meaning of a primitive sign?'

3.262 . . . What is latent in the sign is patent in its application.

On the surface, the name 'Plato' appears to be every bit as much of a simple sign as would any putative name of a simple object. The argument we have just been through, however, implies that it, unlike the names of the simple objects, is to be regarded as a defined sign, with propositions containing the name 'Plato' being broken down in such a way that the name will disappear under analysis. What, then, is the status of the claim, that it is nevertheless a defined sign? Wittgenstein's reply is that if you want to see how a sign functions, you must look at its use, the application of the sign – there are a range of inferential links that a proposition containing the sign will have with other propositions that anyone who understands the sign will

recognize as valid and a range of situations that anyone who understands the proposition will recognize as making those propositions
true. It is such facts as these that will show one how a sign actually
functions. This would also be the reply that Wittgenstein would
make to a criticism that he frequently made in his later philosophy
of the *Tractatus* under the slogan: 'There is nothing hidden'.[26] The
point of the objection is the idea that Wittgenstein, with the highly
complex analyses of everyday language implied by his remarks in the
Tractatus, is digging deep below the surface to uncover a hidden
structure that would explain the surface phenomena, to be thought
of by analogy with physicists positing subatomic particles to explain
what is seen in their experiments. Wittgenstein stresses in his later
philosophy that whatever is significant in the meanings of words
must be something that is apparent on the surface of language, if we
are to use it to communicate. But the analogy I have suggested with
the physicist is misleading. For the author of the *Tractatus* the structures he is uncovering are manifest, if you actually look at the way
people *use* their language. What is more, if Wittgenstein's account is
correct, the speakers of that language have tacit knowledge of these
structures, exhibited in their mastery of the language, their ability to
apply it in practice (cf. 5.5562).

3.263 The meanings of primitive signs can be explained by the
illustrative use of examples. Illustrative examples are propositions containing the primitive signs. They can, therefore, only be
understood if the meanings of these signs are already known.

If we cannot explain the meaning of a primitive sign by a definition –
a verbal explanation, how do we explain to someone the meaning of
such a sign? Wittgenstein's answer is given in what I believe to be the
right translation of 3.263. ('Illustrative examples' is one possible
meaning of '*Erläuterungen*', and is the one that best makes sense of
the present passage.) Suppose we wish to explain to someone the
meaning of a name: we cannot do so simply by pointing at the object
named, since that does not fix the *application* of the name, its rôle in
the language. Therefore we have no alternative but to *use* the name,
that is to say, illustrate its use by producing sentences containing the
name. We must then leave it to chance whether the other catches on
to the meanings of those sentences, which is something that can only
be done by grasping the meaning of the name. At a certain point

verbal explanations of a language give out, and one has no alternative but to *use* the language in the hope that the other will catch on.
(Think here of the way a baby learns language from its parents.)
What this paragraph stresses is the way that you cannot divorce the
meaning of a name from its use in the language, which leads straight
to Wittgenstein's introduction of the 'Context Principle'.

The Context Principle

At 3.3, Wittgenstein introduces the idea, now known as the 'Context
Principle', that was first put forward by Frege in *The Foundations of
Arithmetic*, who laid it down as one of the three basic principles gov-
erning his enquiry, writing:

> Never ask for the meaning of a word in isolation, but only in the
> context of a proposition.[27]

This principle has been widely influential, but at the same time has
been interpreted in very different ways by different writers. In the
case of Wittgenstein it had a central significance in his thinking
throughout his life, and he recurs to it time and again, e.g. quoting
it with approval in *Philosophical Investigations* §49. Despite the
divergent interpretations that have been put upon it, the basic idea
lying behind the principle is clear enough. If we wish to give an
account of meaning, what we wish to understand is what it is to use
language to say or think something meaningfully. But, to say or
think something meaningfully is not to use words or other expressions smaller than a sentence in isolation, but to use a whole sentence. (Of course, we can on occasion say something by uttering a
single word, but that will characteristically be because the word is
elliptical for a sentence, or, as with the word 'Yes', because the word
is used as a whole sentence.) It follows that the basic form of the
account of the meaning of a word should be to explain the contribution that that word makes to the significance of sentences in
which it occurs: if we know the meaning of every sentence in which
a given word occurs, then we know all that there is to know about
the meaning of that word.

(It is sometimes objected to the Context Principle that we can use
words and names meaningfully outside the context of sentences,
for example in dictionaries, or using someone's name to call them:
such objections only affect the letter, not the spirit, of the Principle:

what we want to know from a dictionary is how to use the word
in sentences, which is why dictionaries will typically give the part of
speech of a word, i.e., how to combine the word appropriately
with other words to form sentences; and in the case of using a name
to call someone, the sign we use to call someone would only be a
name if it was also used in sentences to say something about
that person.)

Both Frege and Wittgenstein apply this Principle not only to the
meaning of a word in a broad sense, but specifically to the question:
'What does it mean for a name to refer to something?' We do not
establish the meaning of a name simply by pointing at something
and saying: 'That is called "A" ', since that, taken on its own, does
not explain how to use the name in propositions. If, however, we
know how to use the word in propositions with understanding, then
we know all that there is to know about the meaning and reference
of the name. This leads us on to the topic with which Wittgenstein
follows the Context Principle.

Expressions as propositional variables

At 3.13, Wittgenstein claims that expressions can be represented by
variables that range over the propositions that contain those expressions. If it is only in the context of a proposition that a word or
expression has a meaning, and we understand its meaning to be the
contribution it makes to the sense of propositions in which it occurs,
then we may think of such an expression as having associated with
it a range of propositions, namely the range of significant propositions in which it occurs. There will then be no more and no less to
knowing the meaning of the expression than knowing the contribution that it makes to such propositions, and, provided you know the
meanings of the rest of the expressions contained in the propositions, understanding those propositions.

If, then, we have an expression 'A' that can occur significantly in
the propositions 'F(A)', 'G(A)', 'H(A)' . . ., we could represent it as
a variable '$\Phi(A)$' whose values would be those propositions. Why do
so? There seem to be three ideas worth teasing out.

The first is that seeing the expression as a propositional variable is
simply a way of stressing the Context Principle: if an expression only
has meaning in the context of proposition, then we make that
explicit by showing the expression as a potential constituent of a
proposition in that we present it as an *incomplete* sign, by attaching

the letter Φ to show that it needs supplementation to produce a significant utterance. Frege had contrasted names and predicates as complete and incomplete expressions, in that a predicate needed to have a variable attached to show how it could be completed by a name to form a sentence. Frege's use of variables here was somewhat different from Wittgenstein's, since Wittgenstein's variables range over *all* propositions containing the expression, whereas Frege's range only over those propositions that result from completing the predicate with a name. Also Frege had a further point in mind in regarding predicates and relational expressions as incomplete besides the one that concerns Wittgenstein. He wished to distinguish the relational expression 'ξ killed η ' from the predicate 'ξ killed ξ' [= 'killed him or herself']: the word 'killed' without the variables would not specify which of these was meant. Such a problem could not arise for names, so that specifying the word itself *does* specify the name unambiguously, which gives an additional reason for regarding the name as complete in a way that a predicate is not. Allowing for these differences, Wittgenstein is stressing that there is an important sense in which a name, just as much as a predicate, needs supplementation to be significant – it needs placing in a proposition, and in that sense *all* expressions are incomplete.

The second point is that since the logical form of an expression is given by its ability to combine with other expressions to form propositions, exhibiting it as a propositional variable is a way of showing the logical form of that expression.

He will make the third point explicit at 5.4733, but I believe it is made most clearly at this point. This is his conception of *nonsense*. Suppose we wish to explain why 'Seven is red' is nonsense. What we should not say is that it is nonsense because numbers are not the kind of thing that could be coloured. What we should say, rather, is that when we introduced the predicate 'ξ is red' into the language, we introduced it as a propositional variable ranging over a set of propositions that did not include this sentence as one of its values. Hence the sentence 'Seven is red' does not contain the word 'red' in its familiar sense at all and we have failed to give it any other meaning. Hence the only reason 'Seven is red' is nonsense is because we have failed to give any meaning to some of the words it contains.

I shall postpone discussion of what he says in 3.316–3.317 until I look at 5.501, since these paragraphs have been placed by Wittgenstein at a potentially misleading point in the text. They are misleading not because what Wittgenstein says at the end of 3.314 – that *every* variable can be regarded as a propositional variable – is wrong, but because by this stage he has only introduced one special case of a propositional variable, and he thereby gives the impression that he was making the absurd claim that every variable could be regarded as instances of that special case. In 3.316–3.317 he explains his notion of a propositional variable in its full generality, but it is not until 5.501 that that completely general notion will become important.

Sign and symbol

Wittgenstein has been stressing in various ways that an expression is only the expression it is when considered together with its application in the language. In the light of this, he now introduces a distinction between the 'sign' and the 'symbol'. The sign is what we can perceive of an expression (3.32) – the written marks on the page, say. The symbol is that sign taken together with its logico-syntactic application in the language.

The first point is that the sign, considered simply as a sign and not as a symbol, is frequently ambiguous in natural language – is the sign for more than one symbol, and also that signs that appear on the surface to function in the same way may in fact function quite differently. In both respects, philosophical confusion can easily arise. Wittgenstein therefore (3.325) advocates the establishment of a logically perspicuous notation for the language, in which different symbols would have different signs, and in which there was no appearance that signs which functioned differently could be mistaken for one another.

His second point is one that we have already seen at the beginning of the 'Overview of Themes' chapter of this book: that when we establish the logical syntax for a sign, we may never appeal to the meaning of that sign, but express all the rules *solely* in terms of a description of the expression (3.33). To appeal to the meaning of the sign is to invert the proper order of explanation: since the sign only has the meaning it does when considered together with its syntactic application, until we have laid down the rules for the use of that sign, there is simply no meaning to appeal to.

The final point here is to contrast the accidental and the essential features of our symbolism: it is clear that there is much that is arbitrary about our symbolism, so that different propositional signs could have been used to express the same proposition. Therefore to press through beyond the accidental features to the essential features of the language, we consider the set of all symbols that could do the same job: what they have in common would show what was essential to our language.

Positions in logical space

The final part of this section does not seem to connect naturally with what has gone before. Here the basic idea is that of a proposition picking out a position in logical space. The most appropriate notion of logical space in the present context seems to be one in which the points of logical space are possible ways the world could be; a proposition will then carve out a region of logical space, saying that one of the possible ways the world could be within that region is the way the world actually is. (One may compare this with more modern explanations of the meaning of a proposition in terms of the set of possible worlds in which the proposition is true: the difference is that Wittgenstein is not just thinking of a *set* of worlds, but a structured manifold within which each 'possible world' is located.) Wittgenstein's main point here is that such a determination of a region by a proposition presupposes the existence of the whole of logical space. If this were not so it would be unintelligible that combining that proposition with other propositions should define another, different, region of logical space. Thus, p, q and r each define regions of logical space, but $((p \& q) \vee r)$ will define yet another region of logical space in terms of the regions already defined (3.42).

Topics for discussion

Is it credible that language should be susceptible of the highly complex kind of analysis implied by this and the preceding section?

Many commentators have assumed that by 'indeterminacy' in 3.23–3.24, Wittgenstein meant 'vagueness', where I have claimed he meant 'lack of specificity'? Which is right? Is it possible to make sense of his argument in terms of vagueness?

Spell out for yourself the point and the implications of the 'Context Principle'.

SECTION 4. 'A THOUGHT IS A SIGNIFICANT PROPOSITION'

This section, on the nature of propositions, is in many ways the key to the book. The ideas we look at are: Propositions as true-or-false;

Propositions as pictures; ('The logical constants do not stand in for anything'); Meaning and truth; Propositions as essentially complex (compositionality); Wittgenstein's disagreement with Frege about truth; Understanding as knowledge of truth-conditions; Propositions as showing their sense; Formal concepts; Elementary and non-elementary propositions; Propositions as truth-functions of elementary propositions (Truth-tables); Tautologies; the limits of language; the idea of the general form of proposition and the argument for there being such.

Section 4 may be regarded as the crucial section of the whole book. Here Wittgenstein addresses the question of the nature of propositions and the way they relate to reality, which from the outset had been at the core of his investigations. It is in this section that he establishes the key theses of the whole book, such as that propositions are pictures and that there is a general form of proposition. The rest of the book can properly be regarded as a working out of the ideas of this section.

Wittgenstein, confronted by the question: 'How do propositions relate to reality?' stresses a fundamental difference between the way propositions are related to the world and the way names are related to the world. In his 1913 'Notes on Logic' he had presented an idea that was to dominate his thinking:

> Frege said 'propositions are names'; Russell said 'propositions correspond to complexes'. Both are false; and especially false is the statement 'propositions are names of complexes'.[28]

Frege had assumed that propositions had a reference, and hence could be regarded as (complex) names. He then argued that at the level of reference it was impossible to discriminate propositions more finely than by their truth values: i.e. all true propositions refer to one thing ('the True'), and all false propositions another ('the False'). Behind this section there is a running battle with Frege over precisely this point.

For Wittgenstein, we cannot talk about the 'reference' of propositions at all, since that way of talking failed to do justice to a fundamental difference between propositions and names. Propositions are essentially true-or-false, right-or-wrong, and it is only in virtue of being true-or-false that they can make significant claims about the world. But they can only be true or false if we can understand

67

propositions independently of knowing *that* they are true (4.024). But this implies a radical difference between the way names work and the way propositions work. In the case of a name, you can establish its meaning by correlating the name with some existing feature of the world, so that Wittgenstein can talk at 3.203 of an object as 'the meaning' of a name. However, in the case of a proposition, it represents what it represents independently of its being true. Therefore, if it represents a situation, it must do so independently of that situation actually existing. For this reason, in contrast with the case of the meaning of a name, we may not specify the sense of a proposition by correlating it directly with anything actually in the world.

So the question that this section must answer is: 'How are false propositions possible?', the force of this question being: 'How can a proposition succeed in specifying a non-existent situation?' or 'How can we grasp from a proposition the situation that would make it true, independently of knowing that the proposition *is* true?' The way to approach the 'picture theory of the proposition' is to think of it as providing the answer to *such* questions: a proposition succeeds in specifying a possibly non-existent situation in essentially the same way that a picture can represent a situation both correctly *and incorrectly*.

Wittgenstein now turns from thoughts to propositions, with the claim that a thought is a significant proposition. He begins this discussion with an interlude (4.002–4.0031). This interlude is placed here to forestall the criticism that the description of language that follows does not look at all like what we see if we survey the phenomena of our language, and concerns the apparent deep divergence between the structures that he is to argue are implicit in our use of language and what appears when we look at the everyday propositions we produce in conversation – *these* do not look like pictures or truth-functions of elementary propositions. When he says (4.012) 'It is obvious that a proposition of the form "aRb" strikes us as a picture', your first thought may well be that it is equally obvious that the proposition 'Few people love no one' does not so strike us. Are the structures that he is arguing for just a fantastic mythology grafted onto our everyday language? Here we need to bear in mind the discussion of 3.262 we gave in the last section if we are to find a real justification of the stance Wittgenstein is taking here. The structures that Wittgenstein argued for, which are not visible in the written sentence, are manifest in the *application* of language – e.g. our abilities to recognize valid inferences from our propositions, or to recognize in the concrete case that a particular situation is one that makes what has been said true (cf. 3.326).

If we have these abilities, this shows that the structures of language that Wittgenstein is arguing for are not meant to be 'hidden' in the sense that they are wholly beyond our cognitive grasp, but something of which we have tacit knowledge displayed in the use we make of language, in much the same way that our ability to recognize and to produce grammatical English sentences exhibits a tacit knowledge of English grammar, even if we find it difficult or impossible to give a precise statement of the rules of that grammar. This is the sense in which he can make the extraordinary sounding claim at 5.5562 that everyone who understands propositions at all knows that there must be elementary propositions. As he says (4.002), he is positing here some form of complicated unconscious processing, comparable to that which enables us to speak without any knowledge of how the individual sounds are produced.

There are two points to note here: Wittgenstein's diagnosis of philosophical problems (4.003), and the reference to 'Russell's service' in 4.0031. He introduces here one of the basic themes of the whole book: 'Most of the questions and propositions of philosophers arise because we fail to understand the logic of our language'. In the present context, what he is claiming is that that failure arises because of the divergence between the surface structures of our language – its everyday grammar – and the underlying logical structures. That is how we are to understand the claim that he made in the 1913 'Notes on Logic':

Distrust of grammar is the first requisite of philosophizing.[29]

If we were to devise a notation for our language that accorded with *logical* syntax, then it would be impossible even to formulate the questions and propositions of the philosophers within that notation (cf. 3.325). In that way, those questions would be resolved, not by answering them, but by their vanishing (cf. 6.5). Such a notation would be a *perspicuous* notation for the language, not because it was easier to grasp than our everyday ways of speaking – it would in fact be remarkably cumbersome – but because it would display on the surface the truth-conditions of what we say.

The reference to 'Russell's service' here is almost certainly to Russell's Theory of Definite Descriptions, in which he had analysed such propositions as: 'The present king of France is bald', along the following lines: 'There is a present king of France, and there is at most one present king of France, and if anything is a present king of France then it is bald', arguing that this conjunction had the same truth-conditions as the original. This represented a breakthrough for both Russell and Wittgenstein, because it indicated a way in which the original proposition, despite appearances, was not to be regarded as of subject–predicate form: one could then give a full account of the sense of the proposition without having to suppose that the phrase 'the present king of France' had to stand for something. It further indicated to both Russell and Wittgenstein that there was no need to assume that the surface-grammatical structure of a proposition was a true guide to its logical structure. It has to be said, however, that they were both prepared to countenance far more dramatic divergences between the real and apparent forms of a proposition than this.

Propositions as pictures

The basic claim of the section is at 4.01 – that a proposition is a picture of reality. This will be argued for beginning at 4.02. But between 4.01 and 4.02, he stresses that he is using the term picture in its most general sense, so that he is counting as pictures things that we would not ordinarily think of as such – e.g., the musical score as a picture of a symphony. He argues, however, that in so doing he is not extending the sense of the word 'picture', but that if we reflect on what we ordinarily mean by the word 'picture', these must be counted as such. Certainly when he talks of 'pictures' this will include naturalistic *trompe l'œil* paintings, but we may depart further and further from naturalism and still be talking of pictures: e.g., we may represent the different colours in a scene by different styles of shading and in mediaeval paintings the superior rank of a king could be represented by his being a larger size than the other figures in a painting. What is essential to a picture is that there should be a rule of projection that enables us to derive the situation depicted from the picture (4.0141). As we shall see, (4.04–4.0411) the existence of such a rule implies an idea that we encountered as early as 2.16: the picture and what is depicted possess a common logical form. For Wittgenstein, that is the *only* similarity necessary for us to be able to talk of one thing picturing another.

Now the argument for propositions being pictures is straightforward. When we hear a proposition, possibly one that we have never encountered before, in a language we know, we typically understand what it means without need of explanation (4.02). The crucial part of what we understand is knowing what would have to be the case for it to be true, and, what is more, we can understand it without knowing whether or not it is true (4.024). But that implies that the propositional sign must suffice to specify for us the situation that would make it true: how things stand *if* it is true (4.022). But that can only be the case if the propositional sign embodies for us a rule enabling us to derive that situation from the propositional sign. But in the light of what we have been saying above, that is tantamount to saying that the proposition is a picture of that situation (4.021). This leads on to the idea that language must be compositional.

Compositionality

4.03 A proposition must communicate a new sense with old words.

A language is compositional if the meaning of a proposition is a function of the words it contains together with the way that those words have been put together. This idea was stressed by Frege, who like Wittgenstein, argued that it was necessary to regard our language as compositional in order to explain our ability to understand novel propositions: we understand a proposition with which we are unfamiliar, because it is composed of parts with which we are familiar, put together in a familiar way. But Wittgenstein, besides claiming that compositionality is a necessary prerequisite for language to be capable of expressing new thoughts, also claims that only a language that is compositional is capable of expressing propositions that are true or false. The reason for this is that if a proposition is to be capable of being true or false, it must make sense independently of its being true: we understand it in precisely the same way whether or not it is true, and whether or not we know it to be true. It must therefore make sense even when it is false, so that it must be able to specify the situation that would make it true, even when that situation does not obtain. We build up a model of the non-existent situation, out of elements that stand in for objects that actually exist (cf. 4.031): a proposition is then conceived of as a model consisting of names standing in for objects, and what the proposition means – the situation that would make it true – is then determined by the meanings of those names and the way that they have been arranged: it is in *that* way that a false proposition is possible, and with that a language that is capable of saying things that are true or false is possible.

This seems to work well enough for simple propositions that have no logical complexity, but what are we to say about the kind of logically complex propositions that we use all the time – such as: 'Few people love no one'. Confronted by an example like that, the account we have given so far seems to leave us in the lurch.

'My fundamental thought'

Wittgenstein now introduces what he calls his 'fundamental thought': that the 'logical constants do not stand in for anything' (4.0312). The word that Wittgenstein uses that I have translated 'stand in for' [*vertreten*] is the word that you would use, e.g., for a police reconstruction of a crime, where a policewoman stands in for the victim and a policeman for her attacker. The first sentence of 4.0312 is understood most readily if we consider a simple relational proposition, such as 'John loves Mary'. We may think of this as specifying the situation of John loving Mary, by thinking of it as a simple model, a reconstruction of that situation, where the name 'John' stands in for John, the name 'Mary' for Mary, and the situation of John loving Mary being represented by the fact that these names have been put in a certain relation (standing on opposite sides of the word 'loves'). It is in such a way, Wittgenstein is arguing, that the propositional sign is able to specify the situation of John loving Mary, so that we can tell from that propositional sign what is being claimed.

That account seems, however, only to work for simple relational propositions, or subject–predicate propositions, and it is sometimes claimed that Wittgenstein's 'picture theory of propositions' is only meant to apply to the case of the simplest propositions of all, the 'elementary propositions' (see 4.21 below). It is, however, quite clear that Wittgenstein's argument for the claim that propositions are pictures is completely general, and will apply to propositions of arbitrary logical complexity. To restrict his account to the elementary propositions would miss an essential, if difficult, element in his thought that begins with what he calls his 'fundamental thought'.

For this we need to recall the discussion given in the first section commenting on 1.2. If we consider a logically complex proposition (i.e. a proposition employing one or more 'logical constants' – such words as 'and', 'not', 'some' or 'all'), such a proposition, we said, was never barely true, but if true, always true in virtue of some combination of logically simple propositions being true. Thus, 'John loves Mary or John loves Kate', if true, will either be true in virtue of 'John loves Mary' being true, or 'John loves Kate' being true. But that means that the account that we have given so far of propositions picturing situations does not seem to fit. As it stands, it would only fit if we were to think that there could be a 'disjunctive fact' of *John-loving-Mary-or-Kate*: such a fact would then have disjunction as one of its features, and 'or' would stand in for that feature. But simple common sense tells us that that is the wrong kind of account: that the logical constants don't stand in for anything at all. Therefore if the account of propositions as pictures is to be universally applicable, and not just to simple elementary propositions, we have to give a completely different account of the way the logical apparatus enables a proposition to function as a picture.

Wittgenstein's answer to this is that the logical complexity of the proposition must *mirror* the logical complexity of the situation that it represents – the proposition must have 'the same logical multiplicity' as the situation it represents. This is a difficult idea to bring into focus, so we shall begin with the simple part of the explanation of the phrase before turning to the more complex idea of the possibility of applying the notion of possessing the same logical multiplicity as the situation represented to the case of propositions involving logical constants.

Logical multiplicity

In 4.04 Wittgenstein applies the idea he had introduced at 2.16 for pictures in general to the particular case of propositions: the idea that there must be something in common between a picture and the situation that it represents for it to be possible for the picture to represent that situation at all, whether correctly or incorrectly. In the earlier passage, he talked of 'pictorial' or 'logical' form, but now he uses a different phrase: 'logical multiplicity'. We can see at its simplest what the point is if we consider the kind of case that is most immediately suggested by his wording here at 4.04: suppose that I wish to represent that two objects stand in a certain relation

– that two men are fighting. I may do this in a naturalistic painting that has a range of features in common with the situation it represents. Many of these common features are not essential to the painting representing the relationship in question, and I may instead use non-naturalistic techniques of representation, including the case of the proposition that says that the men are fighting. In such non-naturalistic representations, many of these common features will have disappeared, but there is a range of features that *must* be retained if the picture is to be capable of representing the required situation at all. In particular, since the situation involves *two* men, there must be *two* elements in the representation – each element standing for one of the two men – and since the situation is one of those men standing in a certain relationship, the two elements must stand in a corresponding relationship. In the case of the proposition, the elements will be *names* of the men, and they will be related by their relative positions in the sentence 'A and B are fighting'.

But Wittgenstein's idea of logical multiplicity is far from being exhausted by this kind of headcount of elements: we might for instance consider the case of representing the chronology of a sequence of events by a 'timeline': here temporal relations are represented by spatial relations on a sheet of paper, say. Such a representation is only possible because the line on the page has the same basic topology as the sequence of time: we are able to represent that one event occurred *between* two other events by placing the entry for the one event *between* the entries for the other two. Thus the representation is only possible because we can make sense both of a relationship of betweenness on a line and of a relationship of betweenness in a chronological sequence, and that feature being common to both the representation and what is represented must be preserved, no matter what style of representation we adopted.

4.0411 shows, however, that Wittgenstein is after a more complicated and difficult idea as well – this idea of proposition and the situation represented sharing the same logical multiplicity is to be extended to an understanding of the way in which the logical constants work. In 4.0411 he brings out the way in which the quantification notation must have certain features in order that it should be adequate for the rendering of generality. In interpreting this, we have to bear in mind that this is meant to illustrate the way in which a general proposition must have the same logical multiplicity as the situation it represents. Here we must recall what Wittgenstein means by a 'situation' [*Sachlage*]: a situation consists in 'the existence and non-existence of states of affairs'. Let us suppose for present purposes that [Tom is in the room], [Dick is in the room], [Harry is in the room] etc. are simple states of affairs, in the sense outlined at the beginning of Section 2. These states of affairs can then be modelled straightforwardly by the simple ('elementary') propositions, 'Tom is in the room', 'Dick is in the room', 'Harry is in the room' etc. Suppose we consider now the situations [Someone is in the room] and [If Tom is in the room, Dick is not in the room]. The first situation will exist if and only if one of our simple states of affairs exists, and the second if and only if (either [Tom is in the room] does not exist or [Dick is in the room] does not exist). That is to say, whether or not the situations exist depends upon which combinations of the states of affairs exist. We then represent one of those situations linguistically by producing a proposition that shows us which combinations of truth and falsity for the elementary propositions will make that proposition true, and which combinations will make it false. The function of the logical apparatus is to pick out precisely the right combinations of truth and falsity for the elementary propositions which will make the logically complex proposition true, mirroring precisely the right combinations of existence and non-existence of the underlying states of affairs. The task is to construct a notation that makes this explicit – bringing to the surface the fact that the logical complexity of the proposition reflects the logical complexity of the situation it represents (cf. 5.475). In such a notation, the propositional sign will *show* what the proposition has in common with the situation it represents.

Philosophy as an activity

Proposition 4.1 represents a summary of where we have arrived so far, after which Wittgenstein interpolates a reflection of what this implies for the nature of philosophy. He begins in 4.11 by equating the sum total of true propositions with the domain of natural science. This is one of the very few passages that seems to lend support to those who would see the *Tractatus* as a precursor of Logical Positivism. That, however, is not the purpose of the remark in the present context, and, unlike the positivists, it cannot be his intention to introduce an epistemological criterion into his account of meaning: *that* would be at odds with everything that we have looked at so far. The point is, rather, that if propositions represent the existence and non-existence of states of affairs, then to discover whether they are true or not we must compare them with reality to see whether the relevant states of affairs do or do not exist. But that is the business of empirical enquiry: i.e. of the natural sciences (here construed broadly enough to include what we see and hear in everyday surroundings). Therefore if philosophy is *not* one of the natural sciences (4.111), it cannot be any part of *its* business to put forward propositions (4.112). What is then left to philosophy is not adding to human knowledge by discovering new truths, but simply the clarification of what it is we do know, removing the misunderstandings that created philosophical problems in the first place. He then distances himself, as he would throughout his life, from those who would see any relevance of particular scientific discoveries, such as Darwin's Theory of Evolution by Natural Selection (4.112), to philosophical enquiry.

Does this mean that his conception of philosophy is purely negative, simply destroying confusions? We shall postpone full discussion of this question until Section 7, but for now simply note that it appears not, since he concludes this discussion with:

4.115 It will indicate [*bedeuten*] the unsayable by presenting what can be said clearly.

And with that, he turns to the 'Unsayable'.

Showing and saying

At 4.12 we return to one of the basic themes of the whole book: that the logical form that propositions must have in common with reality, in order to represent it at all, cannot be represented within language, but is manifested, or *shown* by the way language works. In order to say *anything* about reality, language must share a common form with reality; but for that very reason, it presupposes but cannot *say* that reality has that form:

4.12 . . . To be able to represent the logical form, we should have to be able to place ourselves with propositions beyond logic, that is, beyond the world.
4.1212 What *can* be shown *cannot* be said.

This leads on naturally to a discussion of what Wittgenstein calls 'formal' or 'internal' properties of objects and states of affairs: these are properties that it is unthinkable an object or state of affairs should not possess (4.123). If a property is an internal property of an object, to think of that object at all is to think of it as having that property. (One can think of Socrates as wise or unwise, but to think of Socrates is *ipso facto* to think of him as a human being.) In the case of the simple objects that centrally interest Wittgenstein here, the internal properties of an object will be the possibility of its combining with other objects in the appropriate way to form states of affairs (see 2.0121). The possession of such internal or formal properties will then be a paradigm case of something that can be shown but not said: what will *show*, but not say, that an object has a certain formal property, is the range of propositions in which the name of that object can significantly occur. In this way, the formal properties of an object are shown by the use we make of the name of that object.

Formal concepts
In the light of this, at 4.126 Wittgenstein introduces a distinction between formal concepts and genuine concepts.

Let us suppose that one develops, on logical grounds, a theory of categories or logically different sorts of entity – e.g. in Frege's case functions and objects, and in Wittgenstein's case, objects, states of affairs, numbers, etc. – where the mark of the fact that they were *logically* different sorts of entity would be the range of propositions in which the signs for those entities could significantly occur. Then, Wittgenstein is insisting, despite surface appearances, the words we use to designate these different categories – 'object', etc. – do not function as words that designate genuine concepts, and we run into deep philosophical difficulties if we try to treat them as if they did.

This emerges most clearly if we think of *general* propositions which contain words for formal concepts. It looks as though we can say: 'If, from "There are books on the table" we can infer "There are books", so, by parity of reasoning, from "There are objects which are F" we can infer "There are objects" '. Wittgenstein, however, is insisting that 'There are books which are F' is of a different logical form from 'There are objects which are F', and that in a correct logical notation they will receive visibly different renderings. To say that 'There are objects (things)' makes sense is to misunderstand the way the word 'object' functions, and that we are here misled by the surface grammar of such sentences as 'There are objects which are F'. Whereas 'There are objects which are F' is perfectly coherent, 'There are objects' is simply nonsense. 'There are books on the table' will be rendered in quantifier notation as '$(\exists x) (Bx \,\&\, Tx)$', but 'There are objects that are F', not as '$(\exists x) (Ox \,\&\, Fx)$', but simply as '$(\exists x) (Fx)$'.

The rendering '$(\exists x) (Ox \,\&\, Fx)$' would only be appropriate if the word 'object' signified a genuine concept and not a formal concept. As a word for a formal concept, its function is to specify a domain of quantification – and we should read '$(\exists x) (Fx)$' as 'Something is F' and not as 'Some thing is F'.[30] To render 'There are objects which are F' as '$(\exists x) (Ox \,\&\, Fx)$' would only make sense if we were quantifying over a domain which is wider than the domain of objects, but if 'object' signifies a formal concept, there could not be such a wider domain. We may say that a formal concept, such as that signified by the word 'object', is simply the objective correlative of the words 'everything' and 'something'. This is the point of Wittgenstein's saying that 'the expression for the formal concept is therefore a propositional variable'. But if the correct rendering of 'There are objects which are F' is simply '$(\exists x) (Fx)$', then 'There are objects' on its own cannot be rendered, and the apparent analogy between the inference from 'There are books on this table' to 'There are books' and that from 'There are objects which are F' to 'There are objects' is exposed as an illusion.

Hence, Wittgenstein will conclude 'There are objects' is simply nonsense, and that what we want to express by saying 'There are objects' is something that cannot be said, but that is *shown* by the way proper names for objects and variables that range over objects function within the language; what we want to express by saying: 'There are at least two objects' is shown by there being at least two names in the language, etc.

Wittgenstein will now progress to the claim that there is a 'general form of proposition', beginning by introducing the notion of an 'elementary proposition'.

Elementary propositions

When we discussed 4.04–4.0411 above, we argued that Wittgenstein was wishing to explain logically complex propositions as pictures, by showing them as built up out of logically simple propositions. Now, at 4.21, he (somewhat belatedly) introduces the concept of an 'elementary proposition' to designate such simple propositions, which we have already had occasion to refer to. Initially, we may characterize such propositions as propositions that are free of all logical complexity, being capable of being formulated without the use of logical constants. The programme that Wittgenstein has set himself would be to explain the sense of a logically complex proposition in terms of its relation to a set of propositions that are logically simple. However, as we have seen, Wittgenstein is not treating the apparent logical form of a proposition as an infallible guide to its true form. Thus the fact that a proposition *appears* to be void of logical complexity will be no guarantee that we may not discover hidden logical complexity upon analysis. If surface grammatical simplicity does not guarantee real logical simplicity, we need an alternative criterion for what is, and what is not, a genuinely elementary proposition. Confronted by the same problem, Russell, in his version of 'Logical Atomism', had adopted an epistemological criterion at this point: elementary propositions (or as he called them 'atomic propositions') were propositions composed of names of entities with which I was acquainted, and which were beyond the reach of Cartesian doubt. Wittgenstein disagreed: this was the wrong sort of answer.[31] What was required was not an epistemological answer, but one that accorded with grounding an account of meaning in terms of truth-conditions in a set of propositions that engage directly with the specific nitty-gritty detail of what actually goes on in the world, thus explaining how propositions are made true or false by the way the world is. He is therefore proposing as the positive mark of an elementary proposition that such propositions should have a completely *determinate* sense, that is, that they should be utterly specific, and represent precisely one, specific, state of affairs. (See the discussion of 3.23–3.24 above.) Thus the programme now becomes one of explaining the sense of an arbitrary proposition by explaining its relation to the set of elementary propositions, thus conceived.

Truth-tables

In the light of what has been said, since to understand a proposition is to know what is the case if it is true, and it is the elementary propositions that actually engage directly with the world, so that it is their truth and falsity that confers truth and falsity on every other proposition, our task is to represent an arbitrary proposition in such a way as to show which combinations of truth and falsity of the elementary propositions make it true and which, false. Wittgenstein therefore begins in 4.31 by sketching out, in a readily intelligible way, how you can lay out the truth possibilities for n elementary propositions. At least then in the finite case, we can express the truth-conditions of an arbitrary proposition, simply by marking which of those truth possibilities makes the given proposition true, and which false.

This leads directly to Wittgenstein's invention of truth-tables, as illustrated in 4.442 (the example given there symbolises '$p \supset q$'). Truth-tables were also independently invented by Emil Post, as providing a simple technique for deciding the logical status of any formula of propositional logic. (A formula is a truth of logic if and only if it has nothing but Ts in its main column.) When he was asked later about the question of priority in the invention of truth-tables, Wittgenstein said that the question did not interest him, since what he regarded as his discovery was not truth-tables as such, but the possibility of using truth-tables to provide a perspicuous notation for language: the idea being simply that you may replace 'p & q' by the truth-table for 'p & q' – a possibility that he illustrates in 4.442:

4.442 Thus, e.g.,

'p	q	'
T	T	T
F	T	T
T	F	
F	F	T

is a propositional sign.

As Wittgenstein indicates, this may be abbreviated to '(TT–T) (p, q)', or '(TTFT) (p, q)'. If this worked universally as a notation for displaying the truth-conditions of an arbitrary proposition, the next section of this book would be dramatically foreshortened. You could then give the general form of proposition by devising a simple mechanical way of generating for a given n elementary propositions, all the 2^h matrices of Ts and Fs, and that would give you every possible proposition. However, the truth-table notation is only available if there are only *finitely* many elementary propositions. Hence, if he is to leave open the possibility of there being infinitely many elementary propositions, when he is to develop his final account of the general form of proposition, he must replace this truth-table notation by the more powerful N-operator notation introduced at 5.502. As it is, we have here at most a first approximation to a notation for expressing the general form of proposition.

Tautologies and contradictions

The truth-table notation generates two limit, or degenerate, cases that will provide the key to Wittgenstein's account of truths of logic. There is the case where, when a proposition is cast in the abbreviated truth-table notation, there are nothing but Ts in the matrix preceding the list of elementary propositions, and the case where there are nothing but Fs ('tautologies' and 'contradictions'). Since the full account of Wittgenstein's conception of logical truth is given at 6.1–6.11, we shall here just briefly note the points that Wittgenstein makes here. (We may restrict our attention to tautologies, since *mutatis mutandis*, what is to be said here applies also to contradictions.) Firstly, in an obvious way, they are unconditionally true – that simply follows from the way the notation works. Secondly, they 'say nothing' ('I know nothing about the weather, if I know that it is either raining or it is not raining' [4.461]), so Wittgenstein will describe them as 'senseless' [*sinnlos*]. But thirdly, they are not nonsense [*unsinnig*] – they are part of the symbolism (4.4461).

You can see the contrast between 'senselessness' and 'nonsense' by considering that the way the symbolism works allows you to conjoin a tautology and a significant proposition, and the result will be a significant proposition, saying the same as the original proposition ('*p* & taut' = '*p*'), but you do not produce a significant proposition by conjoining a nonsense proposition and a significant proposition, but only nonsense.

Finally, since their 'representational relations to reality cancel one another out', 'they are not pictures of reality'. Saying that they are not pictures appears to put in jeopardy the status of tautologies as propositions, but it is a matter of choice whether we say they are, or are not pictures. We may compare this with the case of an artist producing a series of portraits, each portrait showing less of the details of the sitter than the previous one, until one arrives at the 'minimal' portrait that shows no details at all, and is in fact a blank canvas: it is natural to say the blank canvas is not a portrait, but you could say that it is a limit case of a portrait that is allowed for by the technique of representation that the artist has adopted.

The general form of proposition

Wittgenstein concludes this section by observing that he has now prepared the ground for the topic of the next section: the description of the most general form of proposition, and by briefly indicating an argument at 4.5 why there must be such: the existence of a general form of proposition is entailed by the impossibility of there being a proposition whose form could not have been foreseen.

Before trying to tease out the argument here, there are two points to make about this passage. The first point is that Wittgenstein *is* providing an argument for there being such a thing as the general form of proposition, and not simply assuming it. This is worth saying, since in the *Philosophical Investigations* he gives a highly misleading impression of his earlier position, where when comparing the case of the word 'proposition' to that of 'game', he says:

> Don't say: 'There must be something common, or they would not be called "games" ' – but *look and see* whether there is anything common to all.[32]

When he writes the *Tractatus*, he is *not* simply taking for granted that there must be a general form of proposition in the way he later suggests. The second point is that as in any natural translation, the final sentence of 4.5 looks astonishingly banal, even silly, as a statement of the goal Wittgenstein is struggling to arrive at. Perhaps we should take the overtones of *sich verhälten* that are lost in the English and render it as: 'This is how things are arranged', with the idea, that if we have the general form of proposition, then it will show for any proposition how things must be arranged in the world for it to be true.

The basic spirit of the argument may be brought out if we remember the informal characterization of compositionality that I gave above: 'we understand a proposition with which we are unfamiliar, because it is composed of parts with which we are familiar, put together in a familiar way'. If that it is to have application, then there must be such a thing as '*a familiar way*' in which the parts of the sentence have been put together: in Wittgenstein's words, 'there cannot be a proposition whose form could not have been foreseen (i.e. constructed)'.

If we can understand a novel proposition, without having its sense explained to us, and what is more, if such a proposition makes sense independently of its being true, of what is the case in the world, then it must derive its sense from its position within the system of language. By 'the general form of proposition' Wittgenstein intends the general form of such a system: a system within which every possible proposition will be generated.

Finally, in 4.51, Wittgenstein spells out the way in which settling the general form of proposition will achieve one of Wittgenstein's major goals: setting the limits of language: the general form of proposition will show how it can be constructed out of the set of all the elementary propositions. Anything that cannot be so generated will be thereby shown to be off limits, and therefore nonsense.

Topics for discussion

How strong do you find Wittgenstein's argument for propositions being pictures?

Try to spell out for yourself the argument Wittgenstein briefly sketches for there being a general form of proposition.

SECTION 5. 'A PROPOSITION IS A TRUTH-FUNCTION OF ELEMENTARY PROPOSITIONS'

In 4.5 Wittgenstein had argued that there must be such a thing as 'the general form of proposition': that we could present language as a single system in which every proposition would be generated. In this section, Wittgenstein seeks to implement this by sketching out the basic structure of such a system, and to work out the technical details of his conception of logic. At bottom the formal logic of the Tractatus *is remarkably simple, and this section will be expounded in such a way as to presuppose no detailed prior knowledge of formal logic. Truth-functions; all logic as truth-functional; Operations and functions; Why only one logical constant?; The N-operator; Generality; identity; Solipsism and realism.*

Proposition 5 represents one of the most basic claims of the whole book. The argument for it, in the light of what has gone before, is remarkably simple, and the purpose of this section of the book is to show how it is possible to give a truth-functional account of all the propositions of language. But we must first explain what is meant by one proposition being a 'truth-function' of another set of propositions.

One proposition P will be said to be a truth-function of a certain set of propositions, $\{p, q, r, \ldots\}$, if settling the truth values of every member of the set $\{p, q, r, \ldots\}$ is sufficient to settle the truth value of P. If we then accept that the sense of a proposition is to be given purely in terms of truth-conditions, we may say that P is a truth-function of a certain set of propositions, $\{p, q, r, \ldots\}$, if and only if we can give a complete account of the sense of P by specifying which combinations of truth values of the propositions p, q, r . . . make the proposition true, and which false. Thus, 'p & q' is a truth-function of p and q, since 'p & q' is true if p and q are both true, and false otherwise, and 'it is not the case that p' ('$\sim p$') is a truth-function of p, '$\sim p$' is true if and only if p is false. We can take this truth-functional relationship as giving a *complete* explanation of the senses of 'p & q' and '$\sim p$', and '&' and '$\sim$' are called truth-functional connectives. Whereas 'because' is a non-truth-functional connective, since, although it is necessary for both p and q to be true for 'p because q' to be true, the fact that they are both true does not guarantee that 'p because q' will be true.

There is one further comment to make on this simple notion if we are to understand the use that Wittgenstein is making of it. As usually explained, 'propositional' or 'truth-functional' logic is concerned with the study of truth-functional connectives that join a *finite* number of propositions to form a new proposition (e.g. '&' joins *two* propositions to form a third), and much of the earlier part of Section 5 of the *Tractatus* is explained in ways that really only fit the finite case. However, there is nothing in the notion of a truth-function as just explained that restricts its application to this finite case, and there is no reason why we should not have the case where one proposition is a truth-function of a set of propositions that is *infinite* in number. If we wish to allow, as Wittgenstein clearly does, the possibility that there are infinitely many elementary propositions, then we will only be able to sustain the thesis that *every* proposition is a truth-function of elementary propositions if we admit such infinitary truth-functions. And indeed as the section progresses, Wittgenstein will introduce as his fundamental connective an operator 'the N-operator' where it is essential to his purposes, if it is to do the work required of it that this operator should be an infinitary operator, capable of being applied to a range of propositions, whether that range is finite or infinite in number.

There are, however, several remarks in the early parts of this section of the *Tractatus* that indicate that Wittgenstein had failed to appreciate the radical difference between the finite and the infinite case. This has led many commentators to conclude that the account of logic contained in this section is irredeemably flawed. The truth is that although some of the claims made in the earlier parts of this section are mistaken, it is not too difficult to effect repairs to what he says so as to leave a highly defensible overall picture of logic and the general form of proposition. The most serious repercussions of his failure to pay sufficient attention to the difference between the finite and the infinite case come not in this section, but at 6.122, and I shall therefore postpone further discussion of this until then. For now, I shall simply note in passing points, particularly in the 5.1s, where what Wittgenstein says only holds in the finite case. And because the real interest of Wittgenstein's account lies in the later development of this section, which is indeed applicable quite generally and not just to the finite case, I shall devote most attention here to the 5.5s.

The argument for proposition 5 is really drawing together the threads of what has gone before, and the claim that every proposition is a truth-function of elementary propositions follows immediately from the whole development of the book beginning with its opening paragraphs, together with the explanation of what is meant by an elementary proposition at 4.21. The world has been explained as the *totality* of facts, where the facts consist in the existence or non-existence of states of affairs. The elementary propositions are the propositions that represent these states of affairs, in such a way that there is a one-to-one correspondence between elementary propositions and states of affairs: to every state of affairs there is an elementary proposition that models that state of affairs, and every elementary proposition represents exactly one state of affairs. If, then, we knew the truth value of every elementary proposition, we would know precisely which states of affairs exist and which do not. But we would then know *everything* that is the case, and thus have at our disposal all the information to settle the truth value of any significant proposition whatever: any apparent proposition whose truth value was not decided by settling the truth value of the elementary propositions could not be answerable to the way the world was (cf. 4.26). But saying that is tantamount to saying that every proposition is a truth-function of elementary propositions.

The task of this section is then to devise a notation which will allow us to represent an arbitrary proposition *as* a truth-function of elementary propositions. This will provide a *perspicuous* notation for the language, in the sense that something that is disguised in our ordinary ways of expressing ourselves – the truth-conditions of the claims we make – will be able to be read directly off the propositional sign itself.

Probabilities

The 5.1s need not detain us long. It is difficult to see why Wittgenstein devotes so much space to what must count as a relative side issue: to be sure, any complete account of language must at least indicate how propositions expressing probabilities would be handled within that account, but that does not explain why Wittgenstein devotes more space to them than, say, to the whole of mathematics (6.2–6.241). I shall briefly sketch what the account amounts to, and the difficulties it encounters.

The account goes like this: suppose that we express a proposition as a truth-function of elementary propositions. There will then be some combinations of truth and falsity for the elementary propositions that make that proposition true: let us call a combination that does so a 'truth ground' of the proposition (5.101). Now suppose we consider two propositions 'p' and 'q'. Then if we divide the number of truth grounds of 'p & q' by the number of truth grounds of 'q', that will be the relative probability of 'p' being true, given that 'q' is true.

There seem to be two points about this account worth mentioning:

1. The account has to make the unargued assumption that given any elementary proposition it is equally likely whether that proposition is true or false.
2. This account fails completely if there are infinitely many elementary propositions.

Operations and functions

In the 5.2s Wittgenstein draws a fundamental distinction between 'functions' and 'operations'. First, there is an important terminological point to bear in mind if we are to make sense of what follows, since most mathematical functions will count not as functions but as operations in Wittgenstein's sense, and also, somewhat confusingly, Wittgenstein has retained the traditional terminology of 'truth-functions', even though truth-functions are for him the most important kind of *operations*. To make sense of Wittgenstein's claims in this part of the *Tractatus*, we have to take him to mean by the word 'function' a particular kind of function, namely a propositional function: a function whose arguments are names and whose values are propositional signs. Thus, the function 'ξ is wise' is a function which, for the argument 'Socrates', will have as its value 'Socrates is wise'. Whereas an operation, at least in its primary application for Wittgenstein, will be applied to a proposition to yield another proposition (for instance: 'it is not the case that *a*' applied to a proposition will yield its negation). Wittgenstein's basic point in the 5.2s is to insist that functions and operations, with these notions explained in the way we have just done, work in completely different ways.

Wittgenstein draws out the contrast by saying that functions cannot be iterated, but operations can (5.251). One thinks informally that what this means is that, whereas 'Socrates is wise is wise' (the 'result' of applying the function 'ξ is wise' to one of its values – 'Socrates is wise') is nonsense, 'it is not the case that it is not the case that *p*' makes perfect sense. But Wittgenstein's point is more radical than that. Here we need to bear in mind that a propositional sign is not a complex object, but a fact (3.14). Hence a propositional function is a function that takes names as arguments and has facts as values – namely, facts about those names. That means that a fact is simply the *wrong sort of thing* to be an argument for a propositional function to take as argument. So the point is not that the attempt to iterate a propositional function to one of its values yields the gibberish 'Socrates is wise is wise', but that it makes no sense even to talk about making the attempt. But an operation has at its argument a proposition and as its value another proposition, so that there is no barrier to its iteration.

Truth-operations

Now the idea of a 'truth-operation' (5.3) is easy to understand. A truth-operation is an operation that, applied to a truth-function of a certain set of propositions, yields a different truth-function of the same set of propositions. In the notation of 4.442, where we write '*p* & *q*' as (TFFF)(*p*, *q*), when we apply negation as a truth-operation to this proposition, we get (FTTT)(*p*, *q*): we switch Ts for Fs and Fs for Ts throughout but leave the 'p' and 'q' intact. In general, the result of applying a truth-operation will be simply to change some Fs into Ts, and some Ts into Fs. The result of applying a successive number of truth-operations to a set of propositions will then always be a truth-function of the original set of propositions. The claim at 5.3 is then simply that we can build up every truth-function of elementary propositions, i.e. every proposition, by successive applications of truth-operations to that set (5.32). We will see how Wittgenstein intends to implement that claim at 5.5.

'The one and only general primitive sign in logic'

Wittgenstein wishes to discover a notation that will enable us to see how that proposition has been generated from the elementary propositions by a finite number of applications of truth-operations. But he also wishes to do so using only one primitive sign – the N-operator that he introduces at 5.502 (cf. 5.47). Why does he not want to proceed as Frege and Russell had done, and introduce a number of different primitive signs into his logic? Wittgenstein wishes to give a single homogeneous account of the whole of logic. Suppose you introduce a series of separate primitive signs into your logic as Frege and Russell did – some set such as 'if . . . , then', 'or', 'it is not the case that', 'every', 'some' and 'is identical with'. A number of questions now arise. What have all these disparate ideas got in common? Why do we single out precisely this rather curious ragbag of 'logical constants' as the basic notions of *logic*? How are we to explain the complex network of logical interrelationships between these notions, if they are genuinely distinct primitive notions? There are, for example, many ways in which we can choose *different* subsets of these notions and define the rest in terms of that subset (5.42). What Wittgenstein is claiming instead is that the real primitive notion of logic is the idea of combining propositions together to form logically complex propositions out of them, which given the central claim of this section will mean the general idea of combining propositions to form truth-functions of those propositions: the 'logical constants' of Frege and Russell's logic will then all be explained as special cases of that general idea. He therefore seeks to construct a single piece of logical apparatus (his 'N-operator': see 5.502) in terms of which every possible truth-function of a set of propositions can be defined. This piece of logical apparatus will not in fact be the 'one logical constant' – that will be the general idea of forming truth-functional compound propositions – but since every possible truth-function of a set of propositions can be defined in its terms, it may be used to *represent* that one logical constant.

There is one further specific reason that Wittgenstein has for seeking to construct the whole of logic using only one piece of logical apparatus and that is the concern that lies behind 5.451. We understand the point of this paragraph best if we see its target as Russell and the way the primitive logical constants were introduced in *Principia Mathematica*. Whitehead and Russell first set up propositional logic, introducing 'v' (= or) and '∼' (= it is not the case that . . .) as their two primitive logical constants. At that stage, because they have not yet introduced any signs for generality, they could only introduce '∼' is for combinations of signs that did not involve the use of quantifiers. Then in *9 of the *Principia*, they introduce the quantifiers and have now to explain the significance of propositions that include both one of the quantifiers and a negation sign. They then *define* what such combinations of signs are to mean. Wittgenstein's objection to such a piecemeal introduction of '∼' is spelled out in 5.451. We can simply ask: 'What room is there for a *definition* at this late stage?' Either the negation sign means the same as it did when it was first introduced, in which case the significance of its combination with the quantifiers ought to follow from the way it was initially explained, or it means something different, in which case to use the same sign leads to confusion. Wittgenstein is claiming that this situation can only be avoided if we introduce all the primitive signs of logic, not in serial order, but all at one go. We can do this most simply by introducing only one piece of logical apparatus – the N-operator – and explaining all the supposed primitive signs of Russellian logic purely in terms of that operator.

The Sheffer Stroke

As a preliminary to understanding how Wittgenstein is going to use the N-operator, we need to take a detour via the 'Sheffer Stroke'. Sheffer proved that you could construct all of propositional logic (the part of logic that deals with truth-functions of a finite number of propositions) using only one logical connective. If we take '$p|q$' to mean 'neither p nor q is true', we may show that you can define all the other connectives of propositional logic purely in terms of it. It is quite easy to prove Sheffer's result, but here I shall simply illustrate how other logical connectives can be defined in terms of '$p|q$'. 'It is not the case that p' is equivalent to 'neither p nor p', i.e. '$\sim p$' = '$p|p$' and 'p or q' is equivalent to 'It is not the case that neither p nor q', i.e. '$(p|q) \mid (p|q)$', and so on. Wittgenstein wishes to build up every truth-function of elementary propositions as the result of successive applications of a single truth-operation to elementary propositions. Sheffer's result only concerned truth-functions of a finite number of propositions, but Wittgenstein needs to be able also to cope with truth-functions of infinitely many propositions. He will therefore introduce an infinite analogue of 'neither . . . nor', the N-operator, and assume without proof that Sheffer's result will go through for the infinite case. (It is intuitively clear that it will.) We may think of this infinite analogue as a 'None of . . .' operator, which, applied to a range of propositions (which may be infinite in number), will produce a proposition that says that none of the propositions in that range is true.

Variables as propositional variables

We must return to a claim that Wittgenstein placed misleadingly at 3.314 – that every variable can be construed as a propositional variable. It is not until this point, at 5.501, that he needs the notion of a propositional variable in its full generality, so that his claim and its significance can be properly assessed. What we need to understand is: (1) how that general notion is defined; (2) how every variable can be construed as a propositional variable as thus defined; and (3) why this claim is important to Wittgenstein.

1. By a propositional variable Wittgenstein means a variable all of whose values are propositions. He does not, however, mean a variable ranging over *all* propositions. On his way of using variables, they always range over a restricted domain of propositions. As he says you stipulate the variable by stipulating the possible values it can take and it does not matter how we stipulate its range of values (5.501, cf. 3.316–3.317). At 5.501, he specifies three ways in which we could stipulate such a range, but it is important to note that he does not say that the three ways he stipulates there are exhaustive: in fact for a full implementation of his programme of using propositional variables to handle the whole of logic the list given there would need to be supplemented by yet further ways. A truth-operation applied to a propositional variable as thus explained will yield a proposition that is a

truth-function of the propositions that are values of the proposition. Thus we may take '$V(\bar{\xi})$' to be a truth-operation which, applied to a variable ranging over a set of propositions, produces a proposition that says that at least one of those propositions is true. Then if the variable ξ ranges over two propositions, p and q, '$V(\bar{\xi})$' will be equivalent to '$p \vee q$' and if it ranges over all propositions of the form fx, it will be equivalent to '$(\exists x) fx$'.

2. Although he does not say so, when Wittgenstein claims that *every* variable can be construed as a propositional variable, what he has in mind is the use of variables in standard logic, and not, say, some uses of variables in mathematics such as the differential calculus. We can best understand Wittgenstein's contention by illustrating it. Consider '$(\exists x) fx$'. On the usual understanding of variables, the variable is the letter 'x', and it ranges over objects, and the proposition says that some object has the property f. But we could construe this proposition differently. We could take the variable, not as simply the letter x, but as the complex sign 'fx', ranging over all propositions of the form 'fx', and then reading the proposition as saying that some proposition of that form is true. *Prima facie*, we have achieved the same result, but using only a propositional variable. In such a way, we may replace every use of variables by the use of propositional variables.

3. Wittgenstein's reason for wanting to construe every variable as a propositional variable is simple. He wants to show the whole of logic to be explicable in purely truth-functional terms, and so to set up his logic using only truth-functional operators. However, truth-functional operators always operate on *whole* propositions, and ignore the internal structure of the propositions operated on. It will therefore only be possible to construct a truth-functional operator that can handle the use of variables in logic if the values of those variables are always whole propositions. Therefore he needs to deviate from the normal ways of regarding variables, where the internal structure of propositions cannot be disregarded.

The N-operator

At 5.502, Wittgenstein introduces the N-operator. This is simply the infinitary analogue of the Sheffer Stroke. It is an operator that, applied to a propositional variable, yields a proposition that is a particular truth-function of the propositions over which the variable ranges, namely the proposition that is true if and only if all the propositions of that range are false. Thus, to take the simplest case (5.51), if we let our variable 'ξ' range over just two propositions, 'p' and 'q', then 'N($\bar{\xi}$)' will be equivalent to 'neither p nor q', and if it ranges over a single proposition, 'p', 'N($\bar{\xi}$)' will be equivalent to 'not p'. Sheffer had proved that the whole of truth-functional logic can be defined using only his stroke function as the single logical constant. Wittgenstein is here assuming that the analogous result will hold for infinitary truth-functional logic as well.

His next task will be to show how we can explain the whole of standard Fregean logic using only the N-operator. This naturally breaks down into two parts: explaining general propositions and explaining identity propositions.

Generality

At 5.52, Wittgenstein gives his account of general propositions in terms of the N-operator. Initially, this looks simple and straightforward, but behind this part of the discussion lies a major disagreement with Russell that explains many of the remarks that follow. If we wish to express a general proposition, such as 'Something is f' ('$(\exists x)\,fx$'), using the N-operator, we proceed as follows: we specify a propositional variable ξ as a variable that ranges over all propositions of the form 'fx'. Applying the N-operator to that variable, we produce a proposition that states that no proposition of that form is true: *i.e.* that nothing is f. If we negate that proposition, we obtain a proposition stating that something is f, which is the desired result. Similarly, we can obtain the universal generalization ('Everything is f – '$(x)\,fx$') by applying the N-operator to a variable ranging over all propositions of the form '$\sim fx$'.[33]

Russell, however, more than once presents an argument that convinced him that a truth-functional account of general propositions was impossible, and that would therefore invalidate Wittgenstein's account in particular.[34] The argument runs along the following lines: suppose we wish to give a truth-functional account of a general proposition such as 'All men are mortal'. Then, if we assume that Tom, Dick and Harry are all the men there are, the only way in which we could give such an account is as a conjunction: 'Tom is mortal & Dick is mortal & Harry is mortal'. But this conjunction is only equivalent to the general proposition *on the hypothesis* that Tom, Dick and Harry are all the men there are, which even if true is only a contingent truth. Hence the conjunction is not *logically* equivalent

to the general proposition, and to secure the required logical equiva-
lence we would need to add the clause 'and Tom, Dick and Harry
are all the men there are'. But that clause is itself a general proposition, and hence we have not succeeded in reducing a general proposition to a truth-function of particular propositions. Hence, for
Russell, we need to acknowledge, in addition to the elementary
propositions, at least one unanalysable general proposition, and one
irreducible general fact to which such a proposition is answerable.
This explains one of his first comments that he put to Wittgenstein
when he read the *Tractatus*:

> It is also necessary to be given the proposition that all elementary
> propositions are given.[35]

The thought is that with only the truth-functions of elementary
propositions we would be unable to give an account of general
propositions, and hence we should add at least one completely
general proposition to the list of possible significant propositions.

As he makes clear in his reply to Russell such an addition was
neither possible nor necessary.

1. It was not possible because there was no proposition to the effect
   that a certain set of elementary propositions were all the elementary propositions there were. Suppose we start out with a set of
   elementary propositions, p, q and r say, and ask what we can build
   out of them, thereby setting the limit of what can be said using
   those resources (4.51). What we will 'build out of them' will be all
   the truth-functions of p, q and r. The apparent claim that p, q and
   r are all the elementary propositions is not itself a truth-function
   of p, q and r. It is therefore a transgression of the limits of what
   can said – a nonsensical attempt to say something that can only
   be shown by the way the language works.
2. It was not necessary to add that a certain set of elementary propositions were all the elementary propositions there were. Here we
   need to bear in mind what had been argued in 2.021–2.0212, that
   objects form the 'substance of the world'. The objects of the
   Tractatus are unquestionable, and form a necessary presupposi-
   tion for the existence of language, existing in every world we
   could imagine. Those objects in turn define a set of elementary
   propositions, which are equally unquestionable. Language simply

takes as given a range of objects and with it a range of elementary propositions, without being able or needing to say that these are all the elementary propositions. This is the point of 5.524 appearing in this discussion.

In 5.521, he contrasts his treatment of generality with that of Russell. (He says 'Frege and Russell', but his remarks most directly fit the presentation Russell had given in *Principia Mathematica*.) The opening sentence here stresses his procedure: he separates out two different components in his treatment of general propositions: generality and the truth-function. *First*, we employ the idea of generality by defining a variable that ranges over *all* propositions of a certain form, and then, *second*, we apply the N-operator, as a purely truth-functional operator to that variable. The complaint against Russell in the next two paragraphs has been generally misunderstood, largely because an awkwardness in Wittgenstein's expression of the point has meant that people have misinterpreted what he meant by 'in combination with' (*in Verbindung mit*). What he is here returning to is the complaint we looked at in connection with 5.451. Because Russell did not separate out in the sign for generality a truth-functional component and a component that signified generality, he was obliged to introduce the quantifiers as *new* primitive signs, over and above the signs for truth-functional logic. He therefore saw himself as forced to *introduce* the quantifiers for combinations of signs that included the signs for the logical product and logical sum, creating for Wittgenstein the obscurity he detected at 5.451.

Identity

Wittgenstein next, at 5.53–5.5352, turns to identity. In a letter to Russell written in 1913, he wrote:

> Identity is the very Devil and *immensely important*; *very* much more so than I thought.[36]

Wittgenstein's basic reason for regarding identity as 'the very devil' is clear enough. In 1913, Wittgenstein was already in effect wanting to give a truth-functional account of all logical complexity and hence of the whole of logic, and yet identity seems to provide a clear counterexample to the possibility of doing so. On the one hand, the identity sign seems an essential device in logic, needed for instance to express the proposition that at most one thing is f: (x) (y) $(fx \,\&\, fy \supset x = y)$. On the other hand, truth-functionality is a relation between propositions, and hence if we are to give a truth-functional account of all the apparatus of logic, we must be able to explain all that apparatus in terms of propositional connectives and operations. But the identity sign does not appear to be a propositional connective at all, but the sign for a relation, and indeed the intuitive explanation we would give for identity is that it is the relation that every object bears to itself and nothing else. Wittgenstein has therefore to give an alternative account of identity, and show that that intuitive explanation is simply an illusion. But what follows is not just an *ad hoc* account of identity designed simply to defend his truth-functional account of logic from an embarrassing counterexample, but represents a philosophically interesting train of thought, independently of its use in the development of the argument of the *Tractatus*.

He begins in 5.5302 with a critique of Russell's account of identity: in the *Principia*, Whitehead and Russell had sought to define identity by means of a version of the Principle of the Identity of Indiscernibles. Two objects were explained as being identical if and only if they had all their elementary properties in common – where elementary properties were properties that could be defined by means of truth-functions of atomic propositions (these are the *Principia* equivalent of Wittgenstein's elementary propositions). Wittgenstein begins his own account of identity by rejecting this account (5.5302). His point here is simple: consider the set of all true elementary propositions that contain the name 'a', together with the negations of all false elementary propositions. Substitute for the name 'a' the name 'b' in these propositions throughout, obtaining a second set of elementary propositions and negations of elementary propositions. Now, given the logical independence of the elementary propositions, there is nothing to prevent this second set of propositions being true as well as the first – or at least, this possibility cannot be ruled out on purely logical grounds. If, however, it is logically possible that two *different* objects have all their elementary properties in common, we cannot use such possession of common properties as a definition of identity. Russell was initially devastated by this criticism,[37] but eventually thought the criticism to be question-begging: if his definition was correct, two *different* objects could not have all their elementary properties in common. Although I believe this reply to be inadequate, we will not pursue it further, since this criticism of Russell is only a preliminary to something more interesting, namely Wittgenstein's positive account of identity propositions.

The appropriate starting point for understanding that is Frege's article 'On Sense and Reference'. There he asked how one could explain the difference between the two propositions: 'The Morning Star is the Evening Star' and 'The Morning Star is the Morning Star', where the first registered a significant astronomical discovery, but the second was trivial, even though both names referred to one and the same thing – the planet Venus. He answered that in addition to a reference, we must ascribe to each name a *sense* – a mode of presentation of that reference. Russell, and following him Wittgenstein, glossed that reply by saying that in such cases at least one of the two names could be regarded as an abbreviation for a definite description, so that, e.g., the first of these two propositions could be regarded as equivalent to: 'The brightest heavenly body in the morning sky is identical with the brightest heavenly body in the evening sky'. In this way, every significant identity proposition could be regarded as a proposition in which at least one side of the identity sign was either a definite description or could be regarded as an abbreviation for one.

Then in his article 'On Denoting', Russell offered an analysis of such a proposition along the following lines. Suppose we consider the proposition: 'Scott is the author of Waverley': this may be considered to be equivalent to: 'Scott wrote Waverley; at most one person wrote Waverley; and, whoever wrote Waverley was identical with Scott': '$W(S)$ & (x) (y) $(W(x)$ & $W(y) \supset x = y)$ & (z) $(W(z) \supset z = S)$'. Because of the logical properties of identity, this last clause included by Russell is redundant, and we may consider the analysis: 'Scott is the author of Waverley' $=_{Def}$ '$W(S)$ & (x) (y) $(W(x)$ & $W(y) \supset x = y)$'. This gives us a way of bringing out the informational content of any significant identity proposition. At first sight, however, nothing has been achieved, since both the left-hand side and the right-hand side of this definition use a sign for identity, so that we are explaining identity in terms of itself. But there is a significant difference: on the right-hand side, unlike the left-hand side, the identity sign only occurs within the scope of quantifiers flanked by two variables. What that means is that if we can give an account of *that* use of the identity sign – where it is flanked by variables – we can extend that to an account of every use of the identity sign, since every significant identity proposition can be analysed along the lines indicated into one in which only that use of the identity sign occurs.

What Wittgenstein is proposing is, then, that we replace the use of an identity sign by a convention for reading the variables in quantified formulae (5.532), whereby we only permit *different* substitutions for different variables. This has the effect, e.g., that we may not infer F(a, a) from the formula '(x) (y) F(x, y)', but only F(a, b). Given this convention, 'Scott is the author of Waverley' will now simply be analysed as 'W(S) & (x) (y) ~ (W(x) & W(y))', without any need for an identity sign. What is usually expressed in the form '(x) (y) F(x, y)' will under this new convention be expressed as '(x) (y) F(x, y) & '(x) F(x, x)'. In this way, as Wittgenstein says, it is possible to dispense with an explicit identity sign (5.533).

If we adopt this convention, then certain apparent propositions, such as 'Everything is identical with itself' will not be capable of being expressed (5.534). But since the convention has been argued to be a possible notation capable of expressing *every* significant proposition for which we ordinarily use some form of identity sign, these apparent propositions have thereby been exposed as pseudo-propositions – as nonsense. If, however, they are nonsense, Wittgenstein has provided strong grounds for his claim that identity is not a relation (5.5301): if the identity sign *were* a relational expression, then all of the propositions Wittgenstein lists in 5.534 would have to make sense.

But in the immediate context, the importance of Wittgenstein's treatment of identity in the 5.3s is that he has shown the existence of the identity sign is not a counterexample to his claim that every proposition is a truth-function of elementary propositions, or to his related claim that we can express every proposition as a truth-function of elementary propositions using only the N-operator. We know how to express quantifiers using the N-operator: we simply adapt the explanation of the way in which that is done so as to incorporate the new convention for reading variables.

Intensionality

The topic that Wittgenstein addresses finally in the build up to the general form of proposition is what is called '*intensionality*'. There are various ways in which a proposition occurs as a component of a larger proposition, where it appears impossible to give a truth-functional account of that occurrence. The most familiar examples of this are given by the use of psychological verbs, such as 'A believes that *p*'. Do such propositions not form a counterexample to his claim (5.54) that propositions only occur in other propositions as bases of truth-operations? Wittgenstein's reply is brief to the point of obscurity, but his idea is clear enough. What we must spell out is what he means by its 'being clear' that 'A believes that *p*' is of the form ' "*p*" says that *p*'. Here we must bear in mind his account of *thinking* at proposition 3 and following. For Wittgenstein, for A to believe that *p* is for A to have in mind a picture, a propositional sign that represents that *p*. His claim is then that the claim that A believes that *p* is tantamount to the claim that *that* propositional sign – '*p*' – says that *p*. It is sometimes said that since for Wittgenstein ' "*p*" says that *p*' is nonsense, he is here making the bizarre suggestion that statements assigning beliefs to people are all nonsense.[38] But here we need to bear in mind the distinction between sign and symbol (3.32). When we say of the propositional sign in A's mind that it says that *p*, that is to be compared to the reply we would give to someone who asked of a sign in a foreign language what it said, when we say 'It says "This way to Moscow" ' – which will be a straightforward empirical claim on anyone's account. It is only if we try to say of the *symbol* in A's mind that it says that *p*, that we are talking nonsense on Wittgenstein's account.

When, however, we spell out what it is for ' "*p*" says that *p*' to be true, as Wittgenstein says (5.542), it is a matter of correlating the names in '*p*' with the objects those names are to refer to, not of correlating '*p*' itself with anything. Hence in the fully analysed form of 'A believes that *p*', the proposition '*p*' will not appear. In this way, it is only in the apparent form of the proposition that the proposition '*p*' appears as a constituent of another proposition.

What Wittgenstein says here is sketchy and highly programmatic, but the basic idea, which would need considerably more working out, is clear. Confronted by a case in which a proposition '*p*' seems to be a non-truth-functional constituent of a larger proposition, in the analysed form of the larger proposition '*p*' will always disappear, and we will only have an apparent counterexample to Wittgenstein's basic position.

Solipsism and realism

5.6 *The limits of my language* mean the limits of my world.

This section concludes with what is undoubtedly the most difficult section in the whole book. For once, the difficulty cannot be blamed on Wittgenstein himself: the difficulty is not down to the compression with which the ideas are expressed, but stems from the difficulty in Wittgenstein's wishing to bring us to see something which he contends is unsayable – the 'truth' that he believes the 'solipsist' to be after (5.62). Because of this difficulty, the interpretation that follows is more tentative than most of the other interpretations I give in this guide.

The first question is: 'Why has Wittgenstein placed this excursus on solipsism at this point in the text, at the end of his technical development of the general form of proposition?' The answer is that one of the main points of that development is that Wittgenstein is thereby implicitly setting the 'limits of language': the general form of proposition gives an *exhaustive* account of what can be said, and any putative proposition that cannot be represented as being a truth-function of elementary propositions will be eliminated from the language, simply by not being included. The fact that this is the general form *shows* the limits of language.

The next question is: 'Who is the "solipsist" here?' For this question we need to remember Wittgenstein's background, with his youthful enthusiasm for a form of transcendental idealism, and for Schopenhauer in particular.[39] We may begin here with Kant's statement in the 'Transcendental Deduction of the Categories', where he says: 'it must be possible for the "I think" to accompany all my representations, for otherwise something would be represented in me which could not be represented at all, and that is equivalent to saying that the representation would be impossible, or at least would be nothing to me.'[40] Without getting too involved in the details of the exegesis of Kant here, what this will amount to is that the world, in so far as it is a concern of mine, must be capable of being represented in a single consciousness, subject to the conditions of the possibility of its being experienced by me. In this sense, we may say that for Kant 'the world is my world'. Kant will then go on in the 'Paralogisms'[41] to argue that it is a fallacious inference to think that you have thereby identified an entity that is the metaphysical subject of experience, whereas 'all that I have really in thought is simply the unity of consciousness'. So far this sounds like Wittgenstein, if we transpose Kant's concern for the conditions of the possibility of experience, to Wittgenstein's concern for the possibility of representing the world in *my* language, so that 'the limits of the language mean the limits of *my* world', where once again 'in an important sense there is no subject' (5.631).

Where, then, is the difference? Ultimately, Kant's limits were set *epistemologically* in that when he thought of the world as that about which I could make judgments that were objectively true or false, he was thinking that that entailed that there must be some way in which I could tell in experience whether my judgment was true or false. Because of this he could talk of 'denying knowledge, to make room for faith'.[42] Although our knowledge was restricted to the world as subject to the conditions of the possibility of experience, we could still speculate about the world as it was in itself, as not subject to those conditions. This means that when Kant sets limits to the world of experience, those limits were genuine *limitations*. By contrast, when Wittgenstein talks of the 'limits of language', those limits are set by logic, and here the emptiness of logic comes into its own: the idea of a 'world in itself' to be contrasted to the world as it appears in my language would be the nonsensical idea of an illogical world and 'What we cannot think, we cannot think; we therefore cannot *say* what we cannot think' (5.61). In this way, the 'limits of language' are no kind of limitation whatsoever. Whereas Kant can say that transcendental idealism is compatible with and even entails *empirical* realism, Wittgenstein will conclude that strictly carried through 'solipsism coincides with the *purest* realism' so that the contrast between an idealist perspective on the ideas of the *Tractatus* and a realist perspective simply vanishes.

Topics for discussion

Which remarks in this section would need modification to take account of the possibility of there being infinitely many elementary propositions?

Discuss the disagreement between Wittgenstein and Russell over the possibility of giving a purely truth-functional account of general propositions.

What is it that the solipsist is after which is quite correct (5.62)?

SECTION 6. 'THE GENERAL FORM OF TRUTH-FUNCTION IS: $[\bar{p}, \bar{\xi}, N(\bar{\xi})]$'

Wittgenstein begins this section with a statement of the general form of proposition that he had argued for in the last section by giving a variable whose values would contain every significant proposition. He thereby implicitly defines the 'limits of language': any apparent proposition that could be shown not to conform to the general form of proposition would be thereby exposed as nonsense – as transgressing the limits of language. In this section he then surveys a range of cases of uses of language that, prima facie, *appear from this standpoint to be problematic – either indicating how they would be accommodated, or else how they are condemned as nonsensical. He considers in turn: in the 6.1s, logical truths and falsehoods; in the 6.2s, mathematical propositions; in the 6.3s, scientific theories and causal propositions; in the 6.4s statements of value; and in the 6.5s, metaphysics and claims about the world as a whole, including finally the sentences of the* Tractatus *itself. The theme running throughout this section is 6.37: 'There is only* logical *necessity.' The general form of proposition, which spells out the way in which we can give a systematic account of the truth-conditions of propositions, leaves no room for propositions that are both necessarily true and yet make substantial claims about the world.*

We shall largely concentrate on Wittgenstein's treatment of logical truth and on the consequences of the general form of proposition for metaphysical enquiry, both because these are closest to the overall concerns of the book and because what Wittgenstein says about the other topics and ethics is highly sketchy and at most indicates lines of thought. I postpone looking at the implications of 6.54 until the next section.

In the preceding section, we saw that Wittgenstein introduced the N-operator as a truth-functional operator in terms of which it was possible to define every possible truth-function of a set of propositions. Now, in proposition 6, he gives a formula intended to show how every proposition could be generated out of elementary propositions using only the N-operator. This gives him 'the general form of proposition' – indicating the way in which it is possible systematically to generate *every* proposition as a truth-function of elementary propositions. He also thereby sets the 'limits of language' (cf. 4.51): proposition 6 gives the *general* form of proposition, and hence any apparent proposition that cannot be analysed in such a way as to conform to proposition 6 will be exposed as nonsense.

In this section he will survey the phenomena of language, examining a range of cases that seem, in one way or another, problematic from the standpoint of proposition 6. He will either indicate in such cases how the propositions are to be accommodated, or indicate that we are dealing with forms of words that are only apparently propositions, but which in fact have a different use from saying something true or false, or expose the apparent propositions as no more than that and in fact nonsensical strings of words. At first sight, this might seem an impossible task since proposition 6 is only concerned with how a proposition would look in its fully analysed form, and Wittgenstein is quite clear that he does not know in any detail how the analysis would proceed. Unless we know how we would set about the analysis of any given proposition, how can we know whether or not a proposition could be made, under analysis, to conform to the pattern set out in proposition 6? The answer is that we can have indirect reason to suppose that a given apparent proposition could not be made so to conform. The simplest of those reasons is that proposition 6 leaves no room for substantial necessary truths – the only necessities that can be generated as truth-functions of elementary propositions are the empty truths of logic that we shall look at in the 6.1s. For all their diversity, the propositions that Wittgenstein surveys in this section appear, on an intuitive understanding, to make claims about the world that, if true, are necessarily true, and yet appear not to be empty tautologies. One theme that runs through this section is then what Wittgenstein says at 6.37: 'There is only *logical* necessity'.

But before looking in detail at the different propositions that Wittgenstein will now comment on, we must first look at proposition 6 itself. Wittgenstein unfortunately badly slips up in the statement of this proposition. As a result, a great deal of time has been wasted by commentators, either in trying to make what Wittgenstein says here work as it stands or in arguing that since this cannot be done, Wittgenstein's whole conception of the general form of proposition is incoherent. It is in fact relatively straightforward to identify his mistake, and to correct it.[43] Wittgenstein's notation at this point is intended as a notation for a 'series of forms', as he explained that notion informally at 4.1273 and explicitly at 5.2522.

The account he gives at 5.2522 works perfectly for the case of his explanation of the natural numbers cited at 6.03: $[0, \xi, \xi + 1]$, which yields the series $0, 1, 1 + 1, 1 + 1 + 1, \ldots$, where the second and third terms of the formula give the rule for moving from one number to its successor. However, when he is introducing the notion of an operation, at 5.2521, he says: 'In a similar sense, I talk of the successive application of *more than one* operation to a number of propositions'. Although he only notes it in passing, this extension is essential to Wittgenstein's purposes, since the whole point of his main operator – the N-operator – is that it is not just applied to a single proposition, but to a whole range of propositions, even if that range is infinite in size. That is why Wittgenstein has to define the N-operator not as an operator that is applied to a single proposition to yield a further proposition, but as applied to a propositional variable to yield a proposition. What Wittgenstein overlooks, however, is that this means that his notation for a series of forms is not designed to cope with such an operation. In fact the formula at proposition 6 is radically incoherent. Since the notation is meant to explain to us an iterable process, it ought to give us a rule for moving from one proposition to the next proposition in the series, where the same rule can be applied to the resulting proposition to yield a third term. But Wittgenstein's notation does not do that: instead it gives us a rule to move from a *propositional variable* to a proposition. Hence, having once applied the rule, we cannot simply apply the same rule to the result, but have to proceed in a step-wise manner: specify a propositional variable ranging over some set of the propositions you already know about; apply the N-operator to it, yielding a new proposition; specify a new propositional variable, ranging over a set of the propositions you *now* know about; and so on. There is simply no straightforward way to reduce that process to the simple series of forms that Wittgenstein presumably envisages in proposition 6. What he needs instead is a *recursive* definition of the idea of a proposition, such as the following:

1. If p is an elementary proposition, then p is a proposition.
2. If ξ is a variable ranging over propositions, then $N(\xi)$ is a proposition.
3. All propositions are given by (1) and (2).

Wittgenstein's gloss on proposition 6 at 6.001 says that every proposition is the result of successive applications of the N-operator to elementary propositions. If proposition 6 represents an abortive attempt to do justice to that idea, then this recursive definition does in fact do justice to it. The basic idea is that we start out with the elementary propositions; we then form a new set of propositions by applying the N-operator to sets of the propositions; add this set to the original set of elementary propositions, and repeat the process until we have generated all the truth-functions of elementary propositions. This, as Wittgenstein indicates at 5.32, can be done in a finite number of steps.[44]

In this way, the recursive definition does all that Wittgenstein's proposition 6 was meant, but failed, to do. It presents language as a system within which every possible proposition will find its place, taking as given the elementary propositions, and using only one truth-functional operator. Since the system will contain *every* possible proposition, it thereby implicitly sets the 'limits of language': anything not generated within the system will simply be nonsense.

Or, at least, it does *almost all* that proposition 6 might have been meant to do: it does not generate every proposition in a simple linear series. But it is hard to see what philosophical significance could attach to the possibility of so doing. It is in any case impossible to arrange all the truth-functions of elementary propositions in a linear series – if we allow for the possibility of there being infinitely many elementary propositions: there are simply too many such truth-functions.

'The whole philosophy of logic'

Wittgenstein turns first to the question of the nature and status of the propositions of logic, with the claim at 6.1 that the propositions of logic are tautologies. One of the starting points for the enquiry that was eventually to lead to the *Tractatus* was dissatisfaction with the answer to this question that had been given by Frege, and, above all, by Russell.

> The importance of 'tautology' for a definition of mathematics was pointed out to me by my former pupil Ludwig Wittgenstein, who was working on the problem. I do not know whether he has solved it, or even whether he is dead or alive.[45]

Russell had characterized a truth of logic as a proposition that was both true and completely general. What was meant by this was a proposition that was void of any particular content, and contained nothing but logical constants and variables, such as '$(\exists x)\,(\exists y)\,(\Phi)$ $(\Psi)\,(\sim(\Phi(x, y) \supset \Psi(x, y)) \supset \sim(\Psi(x, y)))$'. Such a proposition would be a truth of logic, if and only if it was true. Wittgenstein's objection to such a characterization of logical truth was clear, and decisive (see 6.1231–6.1233). On the one hand, there is no reason why there should not be completely general, but *contingent*, true propositions about the world; on the other hand, there could be propositions with a particular subject matter that would count as truths of logic just as much as any 'completely general' proposition ('It is not the case that it is both raining and not raining'). What was required was a completely different specification of what it was for a proposition to be a truth of logic – one that would explain why truths of logic were necessarily true, why it was possible for us to know them *a priori*, and why it was unproblematic that they should be necessary and knowable *a priori*. Wittgenstein proposed that such a specification was given by the concept of *tautology*: this is a term that he borrowed from rhetoric, indicating a completely vacuous claim: a proposition that said nothing. The propositions of logic purchased their necessity and *a priori* status, by their complete emptiness, by their failure to give us *any* information about the world. The argument for this specification is simple. If the propositions of logic are necessary and *a priori*, then they are true regardless of the way the world is. But if they are true regardless of the way the world is – of what the facts are – then they can tell us nothing about the way the world is, and they require no special 'logical' facts to make them true. They are actually degenerate cases of propositions, part of the symbolism, but emptied of any content. It is worth noting that Wittgenstein seems to have characterized the truths of logic as tautologies prior to giving the truth-functional account of tautologies: the idea of a degenerate truth-function (a truth-function of a set of propositions that is true, regardless of which combination of truth and falsity you assign to those propositions) is Wittgenstein's way of fleshing out the original idea – that of their complete vacuity.

Against this background, the central train of thought of the 6.1s is straightforward. In fact, Wittgenstein goes badly astray in his development of this train of thought, and subsequent developments in logic have shown that what he says at 6.122 is demonstrably false. This is the point at which Wittgenstein's blind spot – his failure to appreciate the radical difference between the finite and the infinite case – has its most serious consequences. As a result, many commentators have concluded that his whole account of logic must be misguided, and that one must seek elsewhere than in a truth-functional explanation of the truths of logic as tautologies for an adequate theory of logic. But that is far too simplistic a reaction. Although the mistake in 6.122 is serious, and has serious repercussions for some of Wittgenstein's later remarks, the main argument of this section remains intact: it is simply that Wittgenstein draws an overhasty conclusion from that argument.

At 6.113 he claims that what is peculiar about a truth of logic is that you can tell that it is true from the symbol alone, and that that of itself 'contains the whole philosophy of logic'. The argument for this runs along the following lines: the propositions of logic are *necessarily* true. That is to say, they are true regardless of the way the world is. It must therefore be irrelevant to look at the world to find out whether or not they are true (cf. 5.551). A proposition of logic stands in no representative relation to reality: its representative relations to reality 'cancel one another out' (4.462). If, however, the truths of logic are nevertheless true, then that must be because they are true in such a way that it is irrelevant to look beyond the proposition to settle that they are true. But that can only be so if the proposition is itself constructed in such a way as to guarantee its own truth value: hence the symbol in which the proposition is expressed must contain all the information to settle the truth of the proposition. This fact may be disguised in our everyday language in which 'it is not humanly possible to grasp immediately the logic of the language from it' (4.002). If, however, we were to construct 'a sign-language governed by *logical* grammar – by logical syntax' (3.325), the logical form of the proposition would be brought to the surface, and its underlying truth-conditions made explicit. And that means that 'in an adequate notation we would be able to recognize the formal properties of the proposition by simple inspection' (6.122). (It should be noted that he does not claim to have found such a notation, and in particular does not claim that the N-operator notation is such an 'adequate notation'.)

It is only at the last step in this train of thought that Wittgenstein goes wrong. He illustrates his idea in 6.1203 '*in cases in which no quantifiers appear in the tautology*' (my italics) with a remarkably cumbersome notation[46] for propositional logic, where you can tell that a proposition is a tautology by simply studying the notation. In 6.122, however, he claims without further argument that what he has illustrated 'in cases in which no quantifiers appear in the tautology' must be true quite generally.

However, in 1936 Alonzo Church proved that once you progress to the predicate calculus – that is systems of logic that contain formulae with mixed multiple generality (propositions of the form '$(\exists x)\,(y)\,\ldots$') – there could be no decision procedure for such a calculus, no universally applicable algorithm that would enable you to decide whether a given formula was, or was not, a truth of logic. Clearly, casting the proposition in Wittgenstein's proposed 'adequate notation' and inspecting the resulting propositional signs, if this were possible, would constitute precisely such a decision procedure. What, then, are we to say? Clearly 6.122 cannot be allowed to stand. We have to pick our way carefully through Wittgenstein's train of thought here, sorting those parts in what he is saying here that remain highly persuasive from those which must be decisively rejected.

Church's Theorem does not affect the basic idea that in the case of a truth of logic, since consulting the world is irrelevant to determining its truth value, the proposition itself must contain all the information to settle that it is true. Nor does it affect the next step, that we may cast the proposition in a perspicuous notation which brings its truth-conditions to the surface. We may even possibly say that within such a notation the propositional sign will display or *show* the fact that a proposition of logic is such (6.127). What Wittgenstein overlooks is that once he allows the possibility of there being infinitely many elementary propositions, he has also to allow the possibility of quantification over infinite domains. If we then have propositions involving multiple quantifiers ranging over infinite domains, then even the most perspicuous notation may not be able to display the information that a given proposition is a tautology in a form that is surveyable by us. So that even if we continue to say that a tautology *shows* that it is such, it may not do so in a form that is recognizable by us: we may simply lack any method for extracting the fact that it is a tautology. This means that in this use of the concept of 'showing' at least, 'showing' cannot be treated as a straightforward *epistemological* concept.

Wittgenstein's final target here is at 6.127. This may be an idea that he is ascribing to Frege. According to this conception, there would be basic logical truths – logical axioms – and a proposition would be a truth of logic if it was a theorem that could be derived by logical laws from such axioms. On Wittgenstein's conception there is, however, no privileged set of logical truths, or axioms. All the truths of logic are so in precisely the same way, namely by being degenerate truth-functions of elementary propositions. Furthermore, according to that conception every truth of logic is such that expressed in an appropriate notation, the propositional sign itself contains all the information necessary to guarantee its truth and so does not gain its status as a logical truth by its being derivable from anything outside itself.

Here again, we encounter the difficulty raised by Church's Theorem. We may consider 6.1265 to be a half truth. If it only means that a truth of logic contains within itself all the information necessary to settle its truth value, without using an idea of its derivability from other propositions as a criterion of its being a truth of logic, that can be allowed to stand. If, however, as is natural, we take 'proof' to be an epistemological concept, implying that we can always tell whether or not a proposition is logically true by 'calculating the logical properties of the *symbol*' (6.126), we now know that to be false. That implies that axiomatic systems may not be as dispensable as Wittgenstein claims, at least as an *epistemological* tool.

We should conclude this look at Wittgenstein's treatment of logic by considering the question: 'Why was Wittgenstein so convinced from a very early stage that there would have to be a notation that would enable us to tell in every case whether or not a proposition was a proposition of logic?' It is not sufficient here to say that that was what it was natural to think at the time that the *Tractatus* was written, and it is only with hindsight that we regard it as surprising that he should have assumed this. This would not explain Wittgenstein's insistence that this *must* be possible. I believe that it is issues in the philosophy of mind that have betrayed him here. At 4.024 he said 'to understand a proposition is to know what is the case if it is true'. The way that he seems to have interpreted this was to think that understanding a proposition somehow or other involved a parading before the mind's eye of those situations that would have to obtain to make what is said true. If you think *that*, then it will be natural to believe that in the case of the tautology, since there is *nothing* that has to obtain to make what is said true, anyone understanding the proposition will be able to see straight off that it is a tautology. Hence, it will be intelligible that one should make the mistake Wittgenstein makes here (and also that there should be 'no surprises in logic' [6.1251]).

'The propositions of mathematics are pseudo-propositions'

In the 6.2s Wittgenstein turns to the propositions of mathematics, where he seems to have in mind primarily arithmetic and number theory. What he says here looks surprisingly sketchy and inadequate as it stands, and his remarks would need considerable elaboration to constitute a viable philosophy of mathematics. Proposition 6.21 forms an appropriate starting point. The reason for denying that the propositions of mathematics express thoughts is that a thought is a logical picture of facts (proposition 3), and we can make no sense of the notion of there being mathematical *facts* in the sense of 'fact' in which the world is the totality of facts. If to be a significant proposition is to be answerable to the facts, then the propositions of mathematics are not significant propositions. Particularly in view of the opening sentence of 6.2, one might then expect Wittgenstein to advocate some form of 'logicism' – the claim that the truths of arithmetic are disguised truths of logic, and hence, in Wittgenstein's case, tautologies. At 6.22, however, he is clearly differentiating between tautologies and 'the equations of mathematics'. We must therefore turn to his remark about 'equations'.

Although it is true that equations are widespread in mathematics, what Wittgenstein says here is simply not true in general: there are also widespread examples of mathematical claims that are neither expressed as equations, nor can in any obvious way be transformed into equations – consider Euclid's claim that there are infinitely many prime numbers, or, even more simply, inequalities such as '$2^{10} > 1,000$'. This is the first major point at which Wittgenstein's remarks would need elaboration to convert what he says into a viable philosophy of mathematics. What would need to be shown would be the way in which an account of equations could be extended in such a way as to imply a treatment of the claims in mathematics that are not equations.

Next, we need to consider how Wittgenstein is thinking of 'equations' here: the important point, if we are to make sense of what Wittgenstein says, is to realize that by an equation (*Gleichung*), he does not simply mean an identity proposition, such as 'Scott is the author of Waverley'. Identity propositions are certainly not 'pseudo-propositions' for Wittgenstein, but are perfectly significant propositions that will be analysed by Russell's Theory of Descriptions along the lines we looked at in connection with his treatment of identity at 5.53–5.534. (Of course, we might say that on Wittgenstein's account, that these are only apparently identity propositions and, under analysis, their real form is not that of an identity proposition at all.) To understand what Wittgenstein means by 'equations', we need to refer back to 4.241–4.242. There they are described as only 'representational devices' and that is what we need to understand if we are to interpret the claim that they are 'pseudo-propositions'.

It may be tempting to think that by talking of equations as 'pseudo-propositions' Wittgenstein is making the extravagant claim that they are nonsensical. That, however, cannot be his intention, even apart from the wildly counterintuitive nature of the claim that mathematics is nonsense. It cannot be his intention precisely because he goes on to assign them a significant rôle in our traffic with the world. They are also said to 'show the logic of the world', which nonsensical propositions never do. What he must mean is that despite having the apparent form of propositions (being expressed in the indicative mood), they are not true or false, but have a completely different function in our language. What that function is is indicated by the earlier passage at 4.241. There he was concerned to explain his use of equations in expressing *definitions*, which he glossed as 'rules for handling signs' – that is to say '$a = b$ Def.' was to be a rule permitting one to substitute the sign 'a' for the sign 'b'. Now of course, the equations of mathematics are not, or are not all, definitions, but we can extrapolate from Wittgenstein's earlier remarks to understand what he means by a 'pseudo-proposition' in the present context. A definition is typically expressed in the indicative mood and so has the apparent form of a proposition, but is not a proposition that can be true or false: it simply gives us a rule for the use of signs. It is the expression of a rule and is not a proposition, in a way that is analogous to the way in which the sentence: 'Bishops only move diagonally' appearing in the Rules of Chess is not a proposition made true or false by the movements of bishops, but expresses a rule telling one how it is permissible to move bishops when playing chess. So too definitions, and by extension the equations of mathematics, are rules for the manipulation of signs: '$7 + 5 = 12$' is now being seen as a rule permitting one to substitute '12' for '$7 + 5$' when the latter occurs in a proposition. So that from the proposition: 'There are 7 books here and 5 books there', one can move to: 'There are $(7 + 5)$ books here or there', and then the equation permits one to rewrite that as: 'There are 12 books here or there'.

The spirit of Wittgenstein's remarks here is that for him there is only *applied* mathematics or at least applicable mathematics. The equations of mathematics *show* the possibility of inferring one empirical proposition from another, by performing the kinds of manipulations of signs just illustrated, and it is only in so far as they have that rôle that they have any significance whatever (6.211).

Scientific necessities

In the 6.3s, Wittgenstein turns largely to natural science, but also to ways of thinking about, e.g., the will (6.373). What unifies this section is that Wittgenstein is addressing those places where in science and elsewhere it is part of our everyday pre-philosophical thinking to talk in terms of necessities that go beyond logical necessities. The theme that runs throughout the discussion is:

> 6.37 There is only *logical* necessity.

Wittgenstein presumably had Hume in mind when he wrote 6.36311 ('we do not *know* whether the sun will rise tomorrow') and much of the rest of what follows is reminiscent of Hume. Wittgenstein's grounds, however, for the account he gives of science and causality are quite different from anything we find in Hume. In particular, the justification for 6.37 itself is the picture theory (cf. 2.225), with the consequent reflection on the nature of logic that we have been looking at earlier in this section.

We may break Wittgenstein's central claims here down into three stages:

'Metaphysical' principles of science

He begins by looking at certain highly abstract principles that have been thought to be presupposed by science, such as a Principle of Causality or a Principle of Conservation. We may regard what he is doing here (6.32–6.36) as dismantling the Kantian synthetic *a priori*, or at least such principles as those that Kant had argued in 'The Analogies of Experience' were synthetic *a priori* truths.[47] The disagreement with Kant neither takes the form of claiming that such principles are not true, nor that they are not known *a priori*, but that they are in fact vacuous, and tell us nothing about the world – they are actually 'something purely logical' (6.3211). If a Principle of Conservation is left at a purely abstract level ('There is something that is conserved through every change'), then, for Wittgenstein, that tells us nothing about the world, but only something about the form of any possible scientific theory (6.34): *every* scientific theory will incorporate *some* principle of conservation, and if we are prepared to allow our account of *what* is conserved to be sufficiently compli-cated, some such scientific theory will be possible. It is only when we introduce the further demand that it should be possible to give a *simple* account of what it is that is conserved that we start to make substantial claims about the world.

Simplicity

The position then is this: Wittgenstein is saying that the abstract claim that there are causal laws can be reconciled with any possible world that we could imagine (6.362). Scientific method (induction) consists, however, in discovering the simplest set of laws that can be reconciled with experience (6.363). Inductive inferences are not, however, deductively valid. Hence, Wittgenstein will conclude, there is no *logical* justification for assuming that the simplest law that can be brought into agreement with our experience will be true, and he will follow Hume in saying that the acceptance of induction has only a psychological justification (6.3631).

Scientific explanation

At 6.371, Wittgenstein describes the idea that laws of nature 'explain' phenomena as an illusion. How are we to regard laws of nature – laws such as, say, Newton's laws of motion? We have on the one hand Newton's claims proposed as *laws* of nature, and, on the other hand, a vast description, in terms of truth-functions of elem-entary propositions describing all the particular motions of all bodies throughout space and time, where we may imagine that upon examination all these particular motions do indeed conform to these claims. How do these differ? The natural answer is that the laws *explain* all the particular motions that we encounter. But according to the account that we are considering, that is a pure illusion. Newton's laws once analysed in accordance with the general form of proposition will simply be an alternative wording of what is pre-sented to us in a chaotic form by the vast truth-function. The difference between the two will be that the Newton version will be graspable by us, and that is all (cf. 6.361).

Ethics and value

In the 6.4s Wittgenstein turns to questions of ethics and, more generally, of value. Here the reader is particularly strongly advised to read the entries in the *Notebooks* from 14 July 1916 through to the end.[48] The point is not so much that reading these entries makes the position of the *Tractatus* itself clear as that they bear witness to the desperate struggle that Wittgenstein engages in in attempting to hold together two apparently irreconcilable concerns. On the one hand, the central arguments of the *Tractatus* seem to lead to some form of ethical nihilism, but, on the other hand, Wittgenstein wished to take questions of ethics, value and religion with full seriousness. The resulting position is difficult to interpret, and it is open to question whether Wittgenstein succeeds in arriving at a coherent position.

The initial 'negative' claim that there can be no ethical propositions (6.42) is relatively easy to understand: it is a version of Hume's intuition, that you cannot infer an 'ought' from an 'is', translated into the framework of the *Tractatus*. Suppose that we knew *all* the facts, the truth value of every elementary proposition, that still would not in any way dictate what we *ought* to do. Included in 'all the facts' here would be facts about human psychology, human well-being, etc., as much as any other facts. However, what *propositions* are designed to do is precisely state *the facts*, and stating the facts is all that the general form of proposition permits us to do with propositional language.

It is, however, clear that Wittgenstein does not wish simply to stay with this negative conclusion, since he goes on to talk of propositions being able to express nothing *higher*, and the sense of the world as lying *outside the world*. But can any meaning be given to this way of talking? It looks as if Wittgenstein, having rejected transcendental idealism in 5.6–5.64, now wishes to reinstate it, locating the ethical in the will but not in the 'phenomenal' will (6.423). This is highly reminiscent of Kant's 'positive use of the concept of the noumenon'. Consider the following passage from the *Notebooks*:

> The thinking subject is surely mere illusion. But the willing subject exists.
> If the will did not exist, neither would there be that centre of the world, which we call the I, and which is the bearer of ethics.
> What is good and evil is essentially the I, not the world.
> The I, the I is what is deeply mysterious.[49]

If this is a form of transcendental idealism, Wittgenstein has placed himself in an even more precarious position than Kant. Kant's noumenal world was beyond the reach of knowledge, not of thought.

But there are no facts whatsoever beyond the Wittgensteinian limits, and talk of what lies beyond the limits is simply nonsense.

The questions of philosophy

In the 6.5s Wittgenstein finally turns to the range of questions that have typically been thought to be the province of philosophy. That is to say, there seem to be questions of great importance where we can see that no scientific investigation could be of any relevance in answering them: questions that would remain even if all possible scientific questions had been answered and we knew the truth value of every elementary proposition.

> 6.5 If an answer cannot be expressed, neither can the question be expressed.

In the light of the fact that the general form of proposition gives us *every possible* proposition as a truth-function of elementary propositions, then there could be no proposition that could answer a question that was not answered by any possible truth-function of elementary propositions. Hence the main thrust of the 6.5s seems to be entirely negative. As would the Logical Positivists later, what Wittgenstein seems to be saying is that all one can do with such questions as, say, the question: 'What is the meaning of life?' is expose their meaninglessness. We therefore reject all such enquiries out of hand.

Matters are, however, not as simple as that. For in the middle of this discussion we have:

> 6.522 There is indeed the ineffable. This *shows* itself; it is the mystical.

The intrusion of this paragraph in what otherwise looks an unremittingly negative sequence suggests that a purely iconoclastic reading of the 6.5s may not have been Wittgenstein's intention. Another reading is at least possible. When Wittgenstein says, e.g., that the problem of the meaning of life is seen in the vanishing of the problem, that sounds initially as if he is simply saying that the question 'What is the meaning of life?' is simply a silly question, is in fact a nonsensical question, and the question ceases to bother you when you realise that fact. But he also talks here of 'those to whom the meaning of life has become clear', which certainly suggests that they have seen something, and what is more, something more than just that this is a silly question. On this interpretation, what they have seen is something that could not be put into words, but only shows itself, so that part of what they have learnt is a recognition that they cannot say what they have seen. Although the question is indeed nonsensical, the asking of it registers a genuine intellectual worry, a worry that could not be appeased by giving a straight answer to the question, but by seeing something that could not be put into words.

If that was Wittgenstein's intention, then, at any rate, as applied to issues such as the meaning of life, the difficulty is understanding *what* is supposed to show what cannot be said. In the earlier uses of the showing/saying distinction, he was concerned with what was shown by the way our language worked, and where our mastery of the language showed that we were all implicitly aware of what was shown. It is hard to see what takes the place of our mastery of language here.[50]

But maybe Wittgenstein *did* just intend a purely negative reading of these passages. The paragraph which they lead up to is the one which has attracted most attention. Notoriously, at 6.54 he claims that anyone who understands him will finally recognize that the propositions of the *Tractatus* are themselves nonsense. This paradoxical claim has understandably been at the centre of controversy in recent years. The discussion surrounding this paragraph has largely concentrated on the question: 'What implication does what Wittgenstein says here have for the interpretation of the whole of the *Tractatus*?' We shall devote the whole of the last section to surveying the possible answers to that question. Here, we shall conclude this section by drawing together from earlier parts of this book the kind of considerations that lead Wittgenstein to make this apparently outrageous claim.

The conditions for the possibility of language
We may in the first instance think of the *Tractatus* as being a transcendental enquiry into the question: 'How is language possible?', interpreted, at least in part, as the question: 'What must the world be like for it to be describable in language?' (cf. e.g. 2.0211). If we construe the project of the *Tractatus* in these terms we immediately run into a fairly obvious difficulty. Let us suppose that the result of our enquiry leads to the conclusion that for the world to be

describable at all it must be thus and so (a describable world must be one in which *p*, *q* and *r* must all be true). *Saying* this would lead straight to a contradiction, since we can now form the following description: 'a world in which at least one of *p*, *q*, and *r* is false', which *ex hypothesi* would be a description of an indescribable world.

The 'fit' between language and the world

The *Tractatus* is concerned with the way that language relates to reality, the way in which language 'reaches right up to reality' (2.1511), in such a way that, for instance, the particular situation now before me is such that it makes a particular proposition '*p*' true. What we would like to do is to describe the situation now before me in such a way that it is clear that this situation 'fits' the proposition '*p*'. If, however, we wish to specify the states of affairs that make a proposition true, there is no way in which we can do it other than by using precisely the same set of words as those we use in formulating '*p*' itself (or some logically equivalent set of words).

When we talk of 'comparing language with reality', we are talking about something that we learn to do when we learn the language, and which is *shown* by the way that we do in practice compare propositions with the world. But any attempt within language to give an informative description of the relation we are looking for when we seek to verify a particular proposition is doomed.

Formal concepts

When we looked at 4.26, we examined Wittgenstein's insistence on the difference between formal concepts (object, number, etc.) and proper concepts, with his corollary (4.1272) that we could not use '. . . is an object' as a predicate on a par with genuine predicates such as '. . . is a table', and that any attempt to do so would result in nonsense. However, in setting up the distinction, Wittgenstein found himself obliged to transgress his own prohibition. Such claims as he makes at 4.126 turn out on reflection to be nonsense on their own terms.

'6.37 . . . There is only logical necessity'

The only necessary truths allowed for by the general form of proposition are the empty tautologies. The claims of the *Tractatus* itself can scarcely be considered as either contingent matters of fact, made true or false according to which combinations of states of affairs exist, or as empty tautologies. They appear to be presented as necessary *a priori* truths, and therefore to fall outside the scope of the general form of proposition, and hence to be nonsense.

Absolutely general claims
Suppose we start out with the elementary propositions *p*, *q* and *r* and form all their truth-functions. That will give us the limit of what can be said, if those three propositions are the only linguistic resources we have at our disposal. Given those resources, we shall have no way of expressing the idea that *p*, *q* and *r* either are or are not all the elementary propositions there are. That implies that if the general form of proposition is as outlined above, we can form no proposition that is tantamount to saying of a given set of propositions that they are all the elementary propositions. Similarly, we will be unable to say that a set of objects are all the objects there are, or a set of facts are all the facts there are, or for that matter, that the general form of proposition *is* the *general* form of proposition. But it is vital to Wittgenstein's purposes in this book, if he is to set the limits of language, that he should work with the idea of a 'totality of facts' (1.1) and the idea of 'all the elementary propositions' (4.52). His exposition consequently continually strays beyond the limits of what can be said.

What language has in common with reality
Finally, the one thing you cannot talk about on Wittgenstein's account is the one thing he has apparently been talking about throughout the book – the logical form of propositions that they share with reality (4.12).

In all these ways at least, Wittgenstein has apparently been saying things throughout the book which by his own lights cannot be said. The attempt to do so necessarily results in nonsense. In 6.53, he says that 'the only strictly correct method' of teaching philosophy would be a process of Socratic midwifery: you yourself say nothing philosophical, but only attempt to bring the pupil to see that they had failed to give any meaning to some of the signs they had used, whenever they tried to say 'something metaphysical'. In the *Tractatus*, he has, however, clearly departed from this method, and done something that is, on his own account, illegitimate. Where that leaves the way we should understand his book will be our next topic.

Topics for discussion

How damaging, if at all, is it to Wittgenstein's account of logic that there could not be a notation in which you could always tell by 'mere inspection' whether or not a proposition was a truth of logic?
Are 'scientific explanations' explanations?
Is Wittgenstein's account of the ethical tenable?

SECTION 7. 'WHEREOF ONE CANNOT SPEAK, THEREOF ONE MUST BE SILENT'

Although this section of the Tractatus *contains just this one sentence, it is appropriate to devote a whole section to it, since it is the dénouement of the whole of Wittgenstein's thought, and here we draw together the strands of the book that indicate the problematic nature of philosophy, and the central paradox that in the book Wittgenstein has at least apparently being attempting to say what, by his own lights, cannot be said, and hence that his own sentences are nonsense. This is close to the centre of the present debate about the* Tractatus, *and in an introductory guide we do not attempt to adjudicate that debate, but to canvass the different options for interpretation that have been put forward.*

At the end of the last section, we surveyed the different themes in the book that lead Wittgenstein to castigate his own propositions as nonsense, and it is our final task to look at the implications for an understanding of the Tractatus *of the fact that he does so.*

In one way the upshot of the book, as presented in Section 7, is straightforward: having worked our way through the argument, we come to see that it is impossible to present philosophical doctrines – or, at the very least, philosophical doctrines that deal with those questions with which Wittgenstein is centrally concerned in the *Tractatus.* We may leave open for the moment whether this is because we have been brought to see something that can only be shown – 'the limits of language', 'the general form of proposition', 'the essence of the world', etc. – and simultaneously realize that it is impossible to put into words what we have seen, and that any attempt to do so will result in our producing sentences that are nonsense, or alternatively because we have simply been brought in some way to realize that the attempt to talk about such matters is futile, and that even the talk of there being something that can be shown but not said has to be abandoned as an illusion. Either way, 'the problems have, in essentials been finally solved' (Preface, p. 29). We therefore desist from the attempt to construct philosophical theories, and content ourselves with saying only what can be said – 'the propositions of natural science' (6.53). But if in this way the upshot of the book seems straightforward, it is in another way profoundly puzzling.

Wittgenstein has apparently constructed an account of language and the way language relates to the world that resolves all the semantic paradoxes. He has not done so by providing a 'straight' resolution of the paradoxes, but by giving an account of the general form of proposition according to which the paradoxical sentences could not even be constructed, and are simply eliminated as nonsensical transgressions of the 'limits of language'. But in so doing he has led the discussion to a point that is every bit as paradoxical as the original paradoxes: once we have seen what the solution to the paradoxes is we realize that, by the same token, that solution cannot itself be stated. The paradox is clearly exacerbated by the fact that Wittgenstein seems to have been saying precisely what he is arguing cannot be said, and equally we seem to have been able to understand him, and argue for and against the positions he has apparently been putting forward. As Russell says:

> What causes hesitation is the fact that, after all, Mr. Wittgenstein manages to say a good deal about what cannot be said.[51]

We can present the paradoxical situation that the book presents us with by juxtaposing three quotations from it that apparently form an inconsistent triad.

In the Preface, Wittgenstein makes two claims about the *Tractatus*:

> In it thoughts are expressed . . . The *truth* of the truths communicated here seems to me unassailable and definitive.[52]

At 4, we read:

> A thought is a significant proposition.[53]

And at 6.54:

> Anyone who understands me finally recognizes [my propositions] as nonsense.

The tension between these three remarks is obvious. Equally obviously, Wittgenstein cannot be simply careless here, but must have intended to confront us with this tension.

Not surprisingly, there has been considerable controversy as to what to say at this point, and for one group of writers at least, the proponents of the so-called 'New Wittgenstein',[54] everything of importance about the *Tractatus* will turn on the answer we give to this question. Although I believe some version of the fifth of the options that we shall be looking at must be the right way of reading the book, it cannot be the purpose of a study guide to the *Tractatus* simply to present my preferred interpretation. Instead I shall sketch out the different ways of regarding this paradox, and look at the difficulties that confront *each* line of interpretation: it is for the reader to decide which is nearest the truth. *Each* of the following approaches of interpretation faces considerable difficulties, and deciding one of them to be the right one is only a preliminary to the philosophical task of thinking through those difficulties.

I shall first outline five possible reactions, of which the first two are in many ways the most natural, but negative responses. They both in different ways treat 6.54 as a *reductio ad absurdum* – what surer sign that an author has gone wrong than that an author has produced a theory that implies its own nonsensicality? Clearly, neither of these can be Wittgenstein's own position, but equally we should be interested not only in the straightforward exegetical question: 'What did Wittgenstein intend us to take away from the *Tractatus*?', but the further philosophical question: 'How should we react to the book?' The other three represent different strands in the straightforward interpretation of the text. I am deliberately not attaching the names of authors who have commented on the *Tractatus* to any of these, since I am presenting these positions as baldly and simply as possible. If we survey what commentators have actually said, there is considerable variety amongst the interpretations offered, and most will offer qualifications designed to overcome the difficulties that confront us at this point. So we may think of the following as tendencies or directions in which the correct interpretation is to be found, and most commentators will present accounts that are variations on one of the following.

1. Whatever Wittgenstein might himself have thought, 6.54 constitutes a *reductio ad absurdum* of the account of logic and language that he has presented in the body of the book.

2. Rather differently, but once again implying that Wittgenstein has gone wrong, we may challenge Wittgenstein's conclusion that his account does in fact rule out his saying what he has been saying.
3. Although 6.54 was important to Wittgenstein, we may treat it as a relative side issue. There is much that we can profit from or discuss in the earlier parts of the book if we regard the final section of the *Tractatus* as little more than a rhetorical flourish.
4. On the contrary, 6.54 contains the whole point of the book, to which everything else has been leading up. The work has a therapeutic role: you are seduced into reading the work as though it is a theory of the relation of language to reality. Eventually, you come to realize that such a theory self-destructs, and that the propositions that you have been considering condemn themselves as nonsensical. You are thereby disabused of the urge to try to construct such a theory.
5. Wittgenstein is concerned throughout the book with the nature of logic and the relation of language to the world. One of his main concerns is to bring us to see that the answers to the philosophical questions that arise here are things that cannot be put into words – cannot be 'said' – but that are manifest in our use of language. Hence in apparently stating the answers to these questions, he is constantly forced to use sentences to which no meaning can be given. Through the use of these nonsensical sentences – sentences that are condemned as nonsensical by their own lights – he aims to help us to appreciate both what can only be shown, and why what can only be shown cannot be said. Once we have come to see what he is trying to bring us to see – once we understand him – we give up the attempt to *say* what the solutions to our philosophical problems are.

1. A reductio ad absurdum

Although Wittgenstein clearly went into all this with his eyes open, and indeed saw it as one of his main objects to confront his readers with this paradoxical position, whatever he himself might have thought, what we have here is as clear a case as could be imagined of a *reductio ad absurdum*. What could be more absurd than espousing a theory that would, once fully worked out, imply that theory to be nonsense?

Despite the fact that this is a natural reaction that many readers may have, we shall look at it only briefly here. The main thing to say is that, at least as it stands, this is a *shallow* reaction. It should only command respect if it is accompanied by a serious attempt to rebut Wittgenstein's central arguments that lead him to the positions he has been advocating throughout the book. Here it should be noted that the arguments that lead up to Wittgenstein's saying what he does in 6.54 are among the strongest arguments in the book. There are, on any account, many minor flaws in the *Tractatus* and some of the ideas expressed, even if defensible, would not command widespread support. The ideas, however, lying behind Wittgenstein's insistence that there was something that could only be shown and not said are not only among those to which he is attaching most importance, they also have a deep philosophical point that cannot be set aside by any superficial objection.

2. Going metalinguistic

Here we need primarily to consider a suggestion originally put forward by Russell in his Introduction to the *Tractatus*:

> Every language has . . . a structure concerning which, *in the language*, nothing can be said, but that there may be another language dealing with the structure of the first language, and having itself a new structure, and to this hierarchy of languages there may be no limit.[55]

No doubt it was in large part because of this suggestion made by Russell at the end of his Introduction that Wittgenstein reacted angrily when he read the German translation, and condemned what Russell had written as 'superficiality and misunderstanding'.[56] Even if the suggestion Russell is making is 'superficial', it is at least a natural one to consider. In the first introduction of the idea that there is something that can be shown but not said, at 2.172 Wittgenstein claims that if a picture must have something (a form) in common with the situation it depicts in order that it should be able to depict that situation, the one thing that it *cannot* depict is that that situation has that form, since mirroring the form of the situation it depicts is a condition of its being about that situation at all. Instead it mirrors that form. So, in the case of propositions, a proposition will not be able to *say* of the situation it represents that it has a certain logical form in common with the proposition, but will itself display that form. Russell's idea is: maybe a proposition cannot itself say what it must have in common with reality in order to depict it, but why shouldn't *another* proposition say what the first proposition only shows? Generally, if there are certain things which it is claimed a language cannot say, because they are presuppositions of its being able to say anything at all, why shouldn't we be able to say those things in another language that talks about that first language? Wittgenstein only runs into his showing/saying difficulties because he tries to make a language talk about itself as well as the reality it is about. So we replace his way of talking by one that is explicitly about language. Whereas '7 is a number' may, for reasons that Wittgenstein presents, be nonsense, it only appears to make sense because we hear it as saying ' "7" is a numeral', which is a straight-forward empirical proposition *saying* what Wittgenstein claimed could only be shown.

For Wittgenstein himself, this was just a prevarication that missed the point. I shall indicate here the reasons for thinking Russell's response to be inadequate.

Do the metalinguistic propositions succeed in saying what Wittgenstein claimed could not be said?

Do these 'metalinguistic' versions of the problematic *Tractatus* propositions say the same thing as we were trying to say when we put forward the corresponding *Tractatus* propositions? To be sure, ' "7" is a numeral' may be regarded as an empirical proposition, comparable to archaeologists identifying certain marks on a tablet, and saying: 'Those marks are numerals', and we may regard the sentence: ' "Snow is white" is true if and only if snow is white' as a significant proposition about the English language. But to the extent that such metalinguistic renderings of the kind of sentences that we meet in the *Tractatus* make perfect sense, it is an illusion to suppose that they say what Wittgenstein was trying to say with his propositions. Taken in such a way that they are straightforward empirical propositions, these are simply trivial propositions about a particular language. The reason that they can appear to do duty for Wittgenstein's propositions is because we hear them differently. In Wittgenstein's terminology (3.32), we hear them as not about the *sign* '7' – the ink marks on the page – but about the *symbol*, that sign being used with a specific meaning. But if we take the proposition ' "7" is a numeral', as one in which we are talking of the symbol, then '. . . is a numeral' is itself a formal concept, and the sentence is just as problematic as the proposition we started with, and we have got nowhere. Taking a metalinguistic route will always only tell us philosophically irrelevant facts about accidental features of the signs used. Wittgenstein, however, is only interested in the essential logical features of the symbol.

Language or languages?

Russell talks as if Wittgenstein were concerned with the structure of a specific language, so that it then makes sense to talk about discussing that language in a second language. But Wittgenstein's concerns throughout are different: he is asking: 'How is Language possible?' and 'What conditions must be satisfied by any possible language?' In much the same way, when Russell developed *his* theory of types, and the way in which nonsense resulted if one violated type restrictions, he was not concerned with the type restrictions that were recognized by a particular language, but these were intended as restrictions that would have to be respected by *any possible* language capable of talking about sets. If we were to construct a second language to talk about a first, what was claimed to be unsayable in the original language would simply be mirrored as unsayable in the second.

3. Ignoring 6.54

Much of Frank Ramsey's best work was directly inspired by the *Tractatus* and discussions with Wittgenstein, although he wanted nothing to do with the idea that there were things that could be shown but not said. His essays illustrate how much philosophical insight can be derived from a purely straight reading of the *Tractatus*, if you completely disregard Wittgenstein's claim that his propositions were nonsense. Of course, Ramsey was aware that in doing this he was not straightforwardly interpreting the *Tractatus*, but simply profiting from Wittgenstein's ideas where he could. What his example suggests is, however, the possibility of an exegesis of the *Tractatus* that simply ignores 6.54. There have certainly been many commentators who, while not explicitly saying that this is what they are doing, have done precisely that. One may suggest a number of defences of such a procedure. In the first place, it is so eminently possible: there seems no problem in discussing what Wittgenstein says, and arguing for and against it. Indeed, in the second place, there seems no coherent alternative to interpreting the main body of the book as if it all made sense: this is true, even for those who strenuously argue that the whole point of the book is to be found in the fact that its propositions are nonsense: it is only with hindsight, that one recognizes these propositions to be nonsense. In the third place, there is strong reason to believe that there was a version of the *Tractatus* produced in 1916 that would have stopped at proposition 6 rather than go on to proposition 7, with the material now in the 6s as later additions: there is much material in the 6s that is considerably less satisfactory than the earlier parts of the book and much that is difficult to integrate with those parts. Whatever may be said about the passages in which Wittgenstein talks about ethics, a large number of commentators have simply ignored their presence in the book, as peripheral to what is truly philosophically interesting (regardless of Wittgenstein's own evaluation of these remarks): why not treat the 6.5s in the same way? It is here that one runs into the chief difficulty with this approach.

There is a major contrast between the remarks about ethics and the 6.5s. Nothing in the earlier parts of the book would lead one to anticipate what Wittgenstein was going to say about ethics, and indeed it is one of the sections that it is most difficult to reconcile with what has gone before. The ideas that Wittgenstein presents in the 6.5s, and 6.54 in particular, have all been carefully built up to, and emerge, as the natural consequence of the main discussion of the book. When we look through the considerations that I listed in the last section in comment on 6.54, we see that they *all* deal with issues that have been central to Wittgenstein's concerns throughout the book. Unlike Wittgenstein's remarks about ethics, in the 6.5s Wittgenstein is simply drawing out the last consequences of the key positions he has been arguing for throughout the book: if, as he has stressed, one of his aims in setting up the general form of proposition was to establish the limits of language, then that has the consequence that the propositions whereby he established those limits constantly transgressed the limits they were establishing, and thus fell on the wrong side of those limits, and hence were nonsense. It seems we can only ignore 6.54 if we fail to do what Wittgenstein did and do not think our position through to the end.

4. A 'therapeutic' reading
There has been large interest recently in the kind of reading that we now have to consider. This is the so-called 'New Wittgensteinian' reading of the *Tractatus*.[57] In sharp contrast with the preceding

reading, this makes 6.54 the key to the whole book. The book may be thought of as having two components – a 'frame' consisting primarily of the Preface and the 6.5s (6.54 in particular), and the rest of the book included within that frame – where the frame gives guidance to one's understanding of Wittgenstein's whole project. We take with full seriousness Wittgenstein's claim that the propositions in the main part of the book are nonsense, and stress that by nonsense is meant nonsense – gibberish – and that the point of the book is achieved (when the reader finally understands *Wittgenstein*, not the propositions of the *Tractatus*, since there is no such thing as understanding nonsense) when the illusion that those propositions make sense has been dispelled. The book has a 'therapeutic' purpose that seems to run along the following lines: the reader is initially seduced into reading the book 'straight', as an account of propositions and the way propositions relate to reality. This account finally falls apart and turns out to be nonsense in its own terms. Once the reader realizes this, they are disabused of the urge that led them to engage in the kind of enquiry they had apparently embarked on. They then 'see the world aright', in that they return to be content with our everyday language, without the wish to construct a metaphysical theory to underpin that language. The 'traditional' readings of the *Tractatus* have been engaged in a kind of double-think in which they somehow think it is both possible to accept the main tenets that the *Tractatus* apparently propounds *and* that the sentences expressing those tenets are nonsensical. We must take Wittgenstein to have been 'resolute' and that when he talked of 'throwing away the ladder', he meant precisely that – abandon any attempt to find any meaning in the sentences of the body of the book. In particular, we must overcome the illusion that there is anything that can be 'shown but not said'.

This way of interpreting the *Tractatus* derives much of its apparent plausibility from the difficulties in giving a fully satisfactory version of the kind of reading that we shall consider next, which the proponents of this reading call the 'traditional reading'. Without minimizing the difficulties that confront *that* reading, this reading has its own, to my mind, even greater difficulties.

External evidence

At first sight, this reading can look invulnerable to attack, since any paragraphs of the *Tractatus* that seem straightforwardly to contradict this interpretation – such as those in which Wittgenstein stresses that there is that which can be shown and not said (4.121, 4.1212, 6.522) – can simply be jettisoned as rungs of the ladder that must be thrown away. The overwhelming difficulty confronting the 'New Wittgensteinian' reading is, however, the apparent impossibility of squaring it with all the external evidence constituted by the ways Wittgenstein himself talked or wrote about the *Tractatus*: it is hard to find *any* remarks that unequivocally support this reading, but a wealth of remarks that seem to contradict it. This is true whether we consider the *Notebooks* in which he did preparatory work on the *Tractatus*, the ways in which he explained the book to Russell and Ramsey, the developments and modifications he made to the ideas of the *Tractatus* in the early 1930s, or the ways in which he subsequently attacked ideas of the *Tractatus* as ideas he had held earlier. Just to give one example: when he writes to Russell in response to Russell's questions about the *Tractatus*, when Russell had objected: 'It is necessary also to be given the proposition that all elementary propositions are given', he says:

> This is not necessarily because it is even impossible. There is no such proposition! That all elementary propositions are given is *shown* by there being none having an elementary sense which is not given.[58]

This is incomprehensible unless Wittgenstein did indeed believe there was that which could be shown and not said. But it is not so much a question of this or that remark which it is difficult to reconcile with this way of understanding the *Tractatus*; it is the number and diversity of the remarks that are recalcitrant to being read in accordance with it.

What is the 'frame'?
The interpretation rests entirely upon singling out some remarks as 'frame' in which Wittgenstein addresses us *in propria persona* and contrasting those with the other propositions that are to be finally recognized by the reader as nonsense. In practice, the frame is not taken simply to consist of the Preface and the 6.5s, but also to include other paragraphs such as 4.111–4.112 or 5.4733 scattered throughout the book. What is hard to discern is a *principled* account of why these remarks can be singled out, and why Wittgenstein

intersperses them, apparently at random, amongst the 'nonsensical propositions'. This looks a particularly acute problem with, e.g., 4.111–4.112, where on a natural understanding of those paragraphs, they appear as part of the development of a train of thought that begins at 4.1, and as the consequence of an argument that contains propositions that are to be rejected as nonsense. The answer to this problem had better not be that the remarks singled out as belonging to the frame are simply the remarks the interpreters find congenial. Equally, if we read through the sequence from 6.5 to 6.54, which is the sequence that can most easily be read as giving support to the kind of reading we are examining here, we find in the middle of it 6.522 in which Wittgenstein claims that there *is* that which cannot be expressed, but which shows itself. If, according to the 'New Wittgensteinian reading', the 6.5s are intended to give the reader guidance as to the way to approach the *Tractatus*, the sudden incursion of this remark, which must, on this account, be simply thrown away as nonsensical, seems to make the way in which Wittgenstein has organized the paragraphs of the book look crazy. It seems more sensible to look for an alternative way of reading the 6.5s.

How is the 'therapy' supposed to be achieved?
However difficult it may be to fill in the details of the 'traditional' reading that is being rejected by the 'New Wittgensteinians', it is relatively easy to sketch out the main outlines of the way in which according to the traditional reading the book is intended to work: Wittgenstein is wishing to communicate to us something that cannot be put into words, but that is shown by the way language works. To do this, he apparently says what cannot be said, thereby leading us to see what can only be shown: once we have seen what he is trying to draw to our attention, we realize that it could not be properly expressed by the sentences that Wittgenstein had used, and indeed would be falsified by any sentences that purported to say what could only be shown: in fact what has been drawn to our attention condemns precisely the sentences that had been used to draw it to our attention as nonsense. On the account we are now considering there is however a gap in this account – we are shown nothing – and it is obscure what is meant to fill that gap. How are we meant to come to realize that the propositions of the *Tractatus* are nonsense? The only answer seems to be that these propositions, taken

seriously, are in some way self-refuting, or imply their own nonsens-icality. But then there is just as much difficulty confronting this account as confronts the traditional reading in explaining what is meant by 'taken seriously' when applied to sentences that have no meaning whatever – and equally by what it means to talk of such propositions as implying anything. But even apart from that, the fact that sentences are self-refuting or imply their own nonsensical-ity does *not* show them to be nonsense: at most, it shows them to be false.

But even if a satisfactory answer can be given to *those* questions, the real question needs answering: 'How does the fact that the propositions of the *Tractatus* turn out, for what ever reason, to be nonsense have any therapeutic value?' After all, self-refuting meta-physical theories, even theories that turn out to be nonsense in their own terms, are hardly a rarity in the history of philosophy. The Verification Principle in particular was dogged by the difficulty of giving an account of its own meaningfulness in the terms for mean-ingfulness that it itself laid down – and no one has ever seen any therapeutic role for Logical Positivism analogous to the rôle that is here being assigned to the *Tractatus*.

A value judgment

Whether or not this is a difficulty depends upon the judgment one makes on what is of value in the *Tractatus*. It is, however, undoubtedly the main reason why a number of philosophers have not just rejected this reading, but reacted to it with hostility. On any reading Wittgenstein makes a number of mistakes in the development of the *Tractatus*, but those mistakes are comprehensible given that he was struggling with some of the deepest philosophical issues. Anyone reading through the *Notebooks* will be impressed by the intensity of his grappling to get clear about the nature of propositions and logic. And this struggle issues in a whole range of profound philosophical insights that are embodied in the main body of the *Tractatus*. To suppose that he invited us simply to throw all that away in the name of a curious therapeutic exercise can appear as if we are asked to suppose that he committed intellectual suicide. Certainly that therapeutic exer-cise can look remarkably trivial by comparison. It also seems remark-ably ineffective: on his return to philosophy in 1929, he immediately wrote an article[59] in which he continued the kind of enquiry which the 'therapy' would jettison, as if nothing had happened. What is more, he continues that enquiry without even the constant hints throughout the *Tractatus* that there is something problematic about such an enquiry.

5. The 'traditional' reading

I call this the 'traditional' reading, because that is the designation used by the 'New Wittgensteinians' that we have just looked at. However, this designation should not blind one to the fact that there is considerable diversity among the commentators who propose some version of the position that we are now considering: a diversity that is fully intelligible given the difficulties that need to be overcome to give a coherent account of what needs saying here. Indeed, although this is the most natural reading, and indeed the one that best accords, e.g., with the way that Wittgenstein explained his position in correspondence with Russell, the difficulties that confront us here are enormous. In fact, it is only because of these difficulties that the other four ways of reading the *Tractatus* have arisen: they are various ways of cutting the Gordian knot that Wittgenstein presents us with here. (It would be wrong to think that Wittgenstein had himself a neat resolution to the problems that arise here: it is far more likely that he is wanting to confront his readers with a paradoxical situation that he finds just as puzzling as we do.)

According to this reading, there are for Wittgenstein things that cannot be put into words: things that can be shown, but not said. These are things that are manifest in the use we make of language, but which are presupposed to that use of language and cannot be said within language. A major part of the purpose of his book is both to bring us to see what cannot be said, and at the same time to see why it cannot be said. Once we have grasped his point we 'will throw away the ladder'; that is to say, we will recognize that what we have grasped cannot be cast in the form of a metaphysical doctrine, and will recognize that Wittgenstein's own apparent casting of his position in the form of a series of metaphysical doctrines was only a stage that needed to be overcome. He had himself continually been transgressing 'the limits of language' that he wanted us to recognize, and as a result producing sentences that were condemned by those limits as nonsense. Once we understood him, we would give up the temptation to try to say what couldn't be said, and follow his injunction to be silent.

I shall consider two difficulties that confront this reading. These two difficulties are often run together, but they are different and it is well to treat them separately. The 'New Wittgensteinians' have most frequently urged the first, but it is actually the second that presents the more acute difficulties.

Nonsense is nonsense

If we recognize the sentences of the *Tractatus* as nonsense, how can we claim to have more than the illusion of having understood them? If we are 'resolute', to use the 'New Wittgensteinians' favourite term, we will realize that there is no such thing as understanding nonsense, and recognize that the only thing there is for us to do once we have understood Wittgenstein, is to reject the preceding sentences in which Wittgenstein had apparently presented us with an account of the way that language related to reality as gibberish, as only apparently presenting us with anything significant at all. The accusation is that those who maintain that we have been brought to recognize something by the body of the *Tractatus*, or at the very least that Wittgenstein was trying to bring us to recognize something thereby, are committed to the barbarous idea of there being 'significant nonsense'.

The accusation that those who espouse the traditional reading of the *Tractatus* are committed to believing there to be such a thing as 'significant' or 'substantial' nonsense, or at least are committed to believe that Wittgenstein thought there was such is, however, a somewhat malicious caricature. Certainly no one, or practically no one, is going to *say* that there is significant nonsense, so the accusation must be that that is what they are tacitly maintaining, whether they realize it or not. Here we need to keep firmly in mind the distinction between the meaning of a sentence and the use we make of it. The issue is not: 'Does a nonsense sentence have a surreptitious meaning?' but 'Can we use a sentence that is confessedly nonsense to communicate something?' The bald answer to the second question is undoubtedly 'Yes': we can, under appropriate circumstances, use almost anything to communicate something – even pulling someone's nose. But that is too quick. What we are dealing with is *verbal* communication, and what is more, if we learn anything from such communication it is surely only by virtue of the words used, and at least by our apparently understanding what is being said. How is *that* possible? How can we use *nonsense* sentences to communicate? The beginnings of an answer at least are to be found in the fact that we do it all the time. There are countless examples of the figurative use of language where the sentences used are void of any literal sense whatever: to choose an example at random, consider Wemmick's summary of Jaggers in *Great Expectations*:

> 'Deep' said Wemmick, 'as Australia'. Pointing with his pen at the office floor, to express that Australia was understood, for the purpose of the figure, to be symmetrically on the opposite of the globe.
> 'If there was anything deeper', added Wemmick, bringing his pen to paper, 'he'd be it'.[60]

It may be objected that in this case Wemmick is using words with special figurative meanings, and so is not using nonsense sentences, or that when someone speaks figuratively we could, in principle, say what they meant in other words. But both objections rest on crude theories of the possibilities of figuration, and certainly the second objection is question-begging. If the purpose of the use of figuration is to bring us to see something that *ex hypothesi* cannot be said, then of course we cannot give a literal translation of the figure. There is no good reason in general, let alone in this particular case, to suppose that when someone speaks figuratively, what they communicate is necessarily propositional in nature. But this is only the beginnings of an answer: there are countless different types of figuration, and a full answer would require a detailed account of how this particular unusual use of words works.

It is perhaps helpful here to consider what Frege said in a somewhat similar situation to Wittgenstein's. (He had argued for the claim that the predicate '. . . is true' was redundant [i.e. '*p* is true' had precisely the same sense as '*p*'] and that as a result, strictly speaking the word 'true' cannot indicate the essence of logic):

> The word 'true' seems to make the impossible possible: it allows what corresponds to the assertoric force to assume the form of a contribution to the thought. And although the attempt miscarries, or rather through the very fact that it miscarries, it indicates what is characteristic of logic.[61]

Wittgenstein is trying to communicate what cannot be said, and as a result when he says what he does, his words fail to capture what he wishes to communicate, but the way in which they fail, and the very fact that they fail, may be what serves to bring us to see what can only be shown, and why it can only be shown.

What *can 'only be shown'?*
Although great stress has been laid by those who have opposed the traditional reading on the difficulty we have just considered, the far greater difficulty is the second one, which we must now consider. What precisely is it that we have been shown? One thing that it would clearly be wrong to say would be something like: 'If there are infinitely many objects, then we cannot say that there are: we have to be shown that there are'. That is the second caricature of the traditional reading that we sometimes encounter in the writings of the 'New Wittgensteinians'. But *that* is plainly absurd, and may be contrasted with Wittgenstein's own more careful rendering in correspondence with Russell:

> What you want to *say* by the apparent proposition 'There are 2 things' is *shown* by there being two names which have different meanings (or by there being one name which may have two meanings).[62]

Obviously, the question 'What are we shown?' cannot be asking us to say what cannot be said, but it is asking for a characterization of the type of thing that is supposed to be shown to us. The difficulty is that the natural answers – either that our attention is drawn to a fact that cannot be captured in words or to an ineffable truth[63] – both seem to be ruled out by the whole project we have been engaged in. For the world is the *totality* of facts, and the 'limits of language' are coextensive with the set of propositions that are made true or false by those facts. 'Stating the facts' is precisely what language *can* do. Whatever it is that is shown, an additional fact about the world is the wrong kind of answer. It is this question that is the real challenge that confronts us when we read the *Tractatus* (and if we take Wittgenstein's arguments seriously, not simply as a question of exegesis of the *Tractatus*, but as a philosophical question in its own right).

What seems attractive to say is that we are shown not an additional fact, but a pattern *within* the facts, but the difficulty is thinking through what is meant by talking of such a pattern *without* making it an additional fact. Perhaps it was something like this that Wittgenstein himself had in mind, when speaking about internal relations and properties, which for him were a paradigm case of what could only be shown, he wrote:

4.1221 An internal property of a fact we can also call a feature of this fact (in the sense in which we speak of facial features).

Topics for discussion

Which of the above approaches to the *Tractatus* seems to you most satisfactory?

How would you address the difficulties confronting that approach?

Can we use nonsense sentences to communicate something?

What kind of thing is it that can be shown but not said?

At this point, having by now worked through much of the detail of the book, it would be profitable to read the *Tractatus* from cover to cover, asking yourself in particular how well such a reading squares with the answers you give to these questions.

CHAPTER 4

RECEPTION AND INFLUENCE

An account of the reception and influence of the *Tractatus* naturally divides into two parts. There is the influence of the book on other philosophers, but also the fate of the *Tractatus* in the later developments of Wittgenstein's own thought.

ANALYTIC PHILOSOPHY

The first consideration is very general, and does not relate exclusively to the *Tractatus*. At the turn of the last century, a new style of philosophizing emerged, first in the work of Frege, but then that of Russell, the *Tractatus*, F.P. Ramsey, G.E. Moore and later Rudolf Carnap that has come to be called 'Analytic Philosophy' and has dominated much of Anglo-American philosophy ever since. One important way of considering the *Tractatus* is to regard it as one of the founding documents of Analytic Philosophy. Analytic Philosophy is notoriously difficult to define and you can find virtually no philosophical doctrine that would be ascribed to by all philosophers who count themselves as analytic philosophers. Certain trends recur, such as the fundamental importance of logic to philosophy, the need to analyse the language we use in talking about a certain subject matter when approaching the philosophical questions to which that subject matter gives rise; but it is better to consider Analytic Philosophy more as a tradition of influence and a habit of mind than a set of philosophical doctrines, where rigorous argument, precise statement of the positions being argued for, and attention to the language used in formulating philosophical questions are given pre-eminence over the building of large philosophical systems. Although Wittgenstein could never be considered a typical analytic philosopher, part of the importance of the *Tractatus* alongside the work of the other philosophers I have mentioned is that it helped Analytic Philosophy to take shape in the way that it has done.

FREGE

Connected with the previous paragraphs is another consideration, which at first sounds like a backhanded compliment to the *Tractatus*. It was in large part through the *Tractatus* that many of the key doctrines of Frege came to be known to the philosophical community at large. Although Frege is now widely recognized to have been one of the most significant figures in the history of philosophy, for a long time he was generally unknown. It is only after the Second World War, in large measure through the work of Peter Geach and Michael Dummett, that Frege's current reputation became established. During Frege's lifetime, he had a strong influence on many of the most significant philosophers of the time – Husserl, Russell, Wittgenstein and Carnap – but otherwise scant attention was paid to his work. As a result for a long time Frege's influence on philosophical thought was largely indirect, his ideas becoming known through their adoption by these, then much more famous, philosophers. Many key Fregean doctrines are given central significance in the *Tractatus*, and in large measure it is through their appearance in the *Tractatus* that they initially came to have wide philosophical currency. I may mention here the 'Context Principle' (3.3); compositionality (the idea that the meaning of a proposition is a function of the words it contains together with the way they have been put together) (4.03); the explanation of the sense of a proposition in terms of its truth-conditions (4.431); and what has been called 'the linguistic turn in philosophy' (the idea that the right approach to the question, say: 'What are numbers?', was first to ask: 'How do numerals function?', and to answer the first question, in the first instance at least, by answering the question: 'What kind of contribution do numerals make to the meanings of sentences in which they occur?'). Each of these Fregean ideas has been widely influential throughout the twentieth century. They also all have central significance and are given high prominence in the *Tractatus*, even though sometimes Wittgenstein develops these ideas in ways that is different from the way in which Frege himself used them, and, indeed, sometimes in ways with which Frege would have been unhappy. Given that Frege's work was for so long relatively unknown, it would be in large measure through the *Tractatus* that the importance of such ideas became widely known. Mentioning this may seem to belittle Wittgenstein's own achievement, but Wittgenstein was the first philosopher really to appreciate the fundamental significance of these aspects of Frege's work. It does not diminish Wittgenstein's own stature, but helps us to understand his genius and the nature of his work to see him as taking up a range of Fregean ideas in this way and then putting his own interpretation on their significance.

THE *TRACTATUS* AS SETTING AGENDA FOR PHILOSOPHY

Before turning to the specific influence of the *Tractatus* on particular philosophers, such as the Logical Positivists, there is one aspect of the influence of the *Tractatus* that it is easy to overlook, since it may operate unconsciously on philosophers who otherwise had little in common with Wittgenstein, and who would have rejected much of what he said in the *Tractatus*. The *Tractatus* may be seen as having set a new agenda for philosophy, since the importance of the questions raised by the book were recognized even by those who would have been dissatisfied with Wittgenstein's own answers: such questions as the meaningfulness of ethical propositions (6.4f.), the account that could be given of causal necessity (6.37), the possibility of giving an extensional analysis of intensional language (5.541) and, most significantly, the problematic nature of the language of metaphysics. Many of these questions were, in a different guise, already familiar: most obviously, Hume's scepticism about causal necessity was well known. What was new in the *Tractatus* was that these questions were posed in linguistic terms – directed towards the difficulty in explaining certain uses of language.

SPECIFIC INFLUENCES: RUSSELL, RAMSEY AND LOGICAL POSITIVISM

When we turn to the specific influences of the *Tractatus*, we may begin with the two philosophers with whom Wittgenstein had closest dealings during and immediately after the period when he was writing the *Tractatus*. In the case of Russell there is no doubt that, at any rate, at this stage in their thinking, Wittgenstein and Russell each had a significant impact on the other's thinking.

Because much of that impact would have been through direct discussion and conversation it is frequently difficult to know in which direction the influence ran: we *do* know that it was under pressure from Wittgenstein that Russell eventually came to accept that the truths of logic were tautologies, but even there it is unclear whether he understood that in precisely the same way as Wittgenstein. Perhaps the most significant case of mutual influence was the development of Logical Atomism: the interested reader should compare and contrast the *Tractatus* with Russell's account in a set of lectures he gave in 1918, 'The Philosophy of Logical Atomism' which he presents as 'very largely concerned with explaining certain ideas which I have learnt from my friend and former pupil Ludwig Wittgenstein'.

In the case of Frank Ramsey, the influence of Wittgenstein and the *Tractatus* is clear and profound. Ramsey, who died at the tragically early age of 26, had extensive discussions with Wittgenstein and adopted many of Wittgenstein's logical insights into his own work. Many of his best papers owe a clear debt to Wittgenstein and the *Tractatus*, and his major 1925 paper 'The Foundations of Mathematics' is explicitly presented as an attempt to reconstruct *Principia Mathematica* in such a way as to rid it of the defects that Wittgenstein had identified.

In 1927, Moritz Schlick persuaded Wittgenstein to attend discussions being held by members of the 'Vienna Circle', the founders of Logical Positivism. For a time, Wittgenstein had a strong influence on the direction in which Logical Positivism was developed and on the thought of Schlick and Carnap in particular. In this case, however, it is as important to stress where the positivists disagreed as much as where they agreed with the *Tractatus*. First, I should mention the major divergence: the Vienna Circle gave an *epistemological* gloss on the central ideas of the *Tractatus*. The *Tractatus* itself displays virtually no interest in issues of epistemology (cf. 4.1121). In effect, an explanation of meaning in terms of truth-conditions is now replaced with one in terms of verification conditions, and Wittgenstein's elementary propositions are replaced by basic observation sentences. Although this has major repercussions throughout one's reading of the *Tractatus* and many of Wittgenstein's main arguments no longer go through, this misreading was perhaps comprehensible since by that time Wittgenstein had himself come to accept the Verification Principle, and this would certainly colour his own explanations of the ideas of the *Tractatus*. The effect of this shift was that in many ways the version of Logical Atomism that was adopted by some members of the Vienna Circle in many respects had more in common with Russell's account than that of the *Tractatus*. The other big disagreement was over what they regarded as Wittgenstein's 'mysticism' (cf. 6.522): they were appalled by the idea of there being anything that 'could be shown, but not said'. They not only found such an idea completely antipathetic, but also suspected, rightly or wrongly, that metaphysics was thereby being smuggled in by the backdoor. However, despite these differences and despite the fact that their whole approach to philosophical issues was different from Wittgenstein's, we may note the following ideas as influential among at least some of the members of the Vienna Circle. Firstly and most importantly was the rejection of the possibility of metaphysics. The radical empiricism of the positivists already made them deeply suspicious of metaphysics, but what the *Tractatus* gave them was the idea of ruling it out on linguistic grounds: considerations from the theory of meaning would show metaphysical claims to be nonsensical. Coupled with this was the adoption of a conception of philosophy as *analysis* – in their case primarily the logical analysis of the language of science. The other two ideas that are worth mentioning are: (1) the adoption of an atomistic conception of language: the possibility of building up all complex propositions out of a range of basic propositions (though, as noted above, in their case, such propositions would be *epistemologically* basic) and (2) the idea of the truths of logic as saying nothing, although this in their case was glossed as saying that truths of logic were true by convention, or solely in virtue of the conventions of language.

THE *TRACTATUS* IN WITTGENSTEIN'S LATER PHILOSOPHY

Wittgenstein's return to philosophy

In 1929 Wittgenstein returned to Cambridge and his earliest writings when he was there – the article 'Some Remarks on Logical Form' and *Philosophical Remarks* – clearly mark the beginnings of a transition in Wittgenstein's thinking. In the 1929 article he is primarily concerned with the 'colour exclusion problem' – the fact that 'this is both red and green all over' seems necessarily false, but where it looks to be impossible to explain that impossibility using only truth-functional apparatus. He is by then clearly rightly dissatisfied with what he had said in the *Tractatus* itself about this (6.3751) and regarded it as impossible to give an analysis of such propositions that would reveal an underlying truth-functional structure. At this stage of his thinking, he is striving, not to abandon the basic positions of the *Tractatus*, but to modify the *Tractatus* account in such a way as to allow for the possibility of elementary propositions that were incompatible with one another.

In the *Philosophical Remarks*, matters are more complicated, and it is frequently unclear whether he is seeking to adapt the *Tractatus* account or to reject it for something entirely different. The 'colour exclusion problem' continues to exercise him, but a far more significant step towards a rejection of fundamental aspects of the *Tractatus* is his ceasing to believe in the possibility of a purely truth-functional account of generality and the quantifiers.[1] If he was right on this, it would be a far more severe criticism of the *Tractatus* than his worries about the logical independence of the elementary propositions. This would strike at the heart of many of the most fundamental aspects of his earlier book: in particular, he would have to abandon his account of the general form of proposition, and the way in which states of affairs are characterized: as he says,[2] he would now have to admit what he calls 'incomplete elementary propositions' that would presumably no longer be answerable to the existence or non-existence of the kind of utterly specific states of affairs that formed the bedrock of the *Tractatus* account. By comparison, worries over the colour exclusion problem are a relatively minor matter, which could be coped with either by finding a more convincing way of giving a truth-functional analysis of colour propositions, or by modifying the letter but not the spirit of the *Tractatus* account of logical truth.

In the opening paragraphs of the *Philosophical Remarks* he writes:

> I do not now have phenomenological language, or 'primary language' as I called it, in mind as my goal. I no longer hold it to be necessary. All that is possible and necessary is to separate what is essential from what is inessential in *our* language.[3]

Although he refers here to 'phenomenological language'[4] rather than the fully analysed form of language of the *Tractatus*, these remarks would carry over *mutatis mutandis* to the *Tractatus* itself. These remarks, considered in isolation, would suggest that he is starting to do philosophy in a completely new way. Much, however, remains radically unclear, giving the impression that Wittgenstein is at that stage floundering: uncertain whether he is trying to modify the *Tractatus* or to reject it and replace his earlier approach with something quite different, and if so, what.

It is in the writings following the *Philosophical Remarks* – the *Philosophical Grammar* and the *Big Typescript* – that some of the characteristic positions of his later philosophy begin to emerge, and concern with the ideas of the *Tractatus* gradually move more and more into the background. It is in the *Philosophical Investigations* that he next confronts the ideas of the *Tractatus*.

The Tractatus *in the* Philosophical Investigations

When the *Philosophical Investigations* first came out, it had a disastrous effect on the reputation of the *Tractatus*. In the Preface, Wittgenstein says:

> For since beginning to occupy myself with philosophy again, sixteen years ago, I have been forced to recognize grave mistakes in what I wrote in that first book.[5]

He then, in the early paragraphs of the book, subjects a series of doctrines of the *Tractatus* to sustained criticism. Although the *Tractatus* is only occasionally mentioned explicitly,[6] these paragraphs certainly read like a dismantling of the most characteristic ideas of his earlier book. Because of this, the attitude arose that the *Tractatus* should be regarded as of largely historical interest: what worse advertisement for a book than that its own author disowned its basic positions? And in so far as there were continuities between his earlier and later work, they would be better preserved in the later work once they had been freed from the now discredited accompaniments. However, things are much more complicated than this would suggest, and in the process many of the deepest insights of his early work were in danger of being completely overlooked and lost.

Let us first consider the question of the continuities and discontinuities in his philosophy. Here one can discover the whole gamut of interpretations, from those who see the *Investigations* as simply rejecting his earlier philosophy as an example of the kind of mythological fantasy that philosophers are prone to produce, to those who stress deep continuities. I myself used to believe the discontinuities to be less than I now do. The following seems safe: Wittgenstein continues to believe that philosophical problems arise because we misunderstand the way language works, and that those problems are dissolved by careful attention to the way that language does in fact work. However, his conception of language has undergone a radical change, and as a consequence, discovering the way language does in fact work can no longer be a matter of uncovering an underlying logical structure to that language, but instead takes the form of a far more piecemeal examination of the language involved in particular philosophical disputes: above all, he explicitly rejects one of the most crucial features of the *Tractatus*, the idea of there being a 'general form of proposition' (*Investigations*, §65). On many other key issues – whether he still regards propositions as pictures, or holds that there is that which can be shown but not said – he is simply silent.

The criticisms of the *Tractatus* in the early paragraphs, if they are indeed intended as such, are highly puzzling: they so frequently look so weak. The actual positions of the *Tractatus* seem to be caricatured, and the actual arguments he had presented for those positions either simply not considered, or again presented in the form of a crude caricature. The arguments he then presents against those positions typically only work against the caricature. Consider one of the worst examples: in §48 he presents a matrix of coloured squares as an example of a proposition for which 'the account in the *Theaetetus*', and by implication (§46) his own account of an elementary proposition, 'is really valid'. But this matrix satisfies *none* of the conditions he had actually laid down for an elementary proposition,[7] and his subsequent discussion of the example only presents criticisms that work against the example in ways in which it differs from the way an actual elementary proposition would be. Such passages give the strong impression that, over twenty years after the event, during which time he had been thinking along such different lines, Wittgenstein could no longer fully recover what he had said earlier, or why he had said it.

It may, however, be that for the most part Wittgenstein was more interested in discussing a position than in the question whether that was in fact his earlier position. There is, however, one case where this is not so: this is his rejection of there being a general form of proposition (§65). Once again, he does not address the argument he had presented in the *Tractatus* for the existence of a general form (4.5), but seems to treat it as if it were an unthinking assumption he had made earlier. What he does in the *Investigations* is simply parade before us the extraordinary diversity of uses of language that there are, and invites us to ask whether it is credible that they should all conform to a simple underlying pattern, such as he had envisaged in the *Tractatus* (§§18, 23). Here it seems to me a strong case can be made out for saying that his first thought may be nearer the truth than his later one. This is not the place to argue this in full, but I will indicate two considerations to think about. Firstly, Wittgenstein in the *Investigations* makes *no* distinction between what a sentence means, and the use to which we put it, and much of the diversity he illustrates in §23 is diversity, in use not meaning. Secondly, it is more than arguable that unless there was a simple underlying system to the language, it would lack the flexibility necessary for it to be capable of being put to such diverse uses. Whether I am right or wrong about Wittgenstein's criticisms of the *Tractatus* here, the reader should not simply assume that in every case where they disagree, the later philosophy is right and the earlier philosophy wrong. No one will believe that Wittgenstein got *everything* right in the *Tractatus*. But if you simply assume that his earlier work is superseded by the *Investigations*, you are in danger of losing many deep insights that are not done full justice in his later work. It is, in any case, important not to treat Wittgenstein as infallible in the interpretations of the *Tractatus* he gives in the *Investigations*, but to test what he says against the actual text of the *Tractatus* itself.

It may be that it is in fact in the later parts of the *Investigations*, when the *Tractatus* is not explicitly referred to, that there is the deepest and most penetrating engagement with the *Tractatus*. In the *Tractatus*, Wittgenstein seems to have assumed a simple philosophy of mind, wherein to understand the claim that *p* was to have in one's mind (maybe unconsciously) a parade of the situations that would make '*p*' true. Although this is very much in the background, it is, I believe, necessary to assume this to make sense of some of the things that he says. (Including possibly his assumption that there *must* be a decision procedure for the whole of logic – cf. 6.122.) It may be this way of thinking of understanding that is one of the targets of such remarks as: 'Try not to think of understanding as a "mental process" at all'. (Notice the final paragraph of §81.) At least one profitable way of viewing the later discussions of mental phenomena, including the 'Private Language Argument', is to see Wittgenstein as seeking to free himself from a way of thinking about the mental that he had adopted earlier.

CHAPTER 5

GUIDE TO FURTHER READING

(For bibliographical details of works that follow, see Bibliography.)

1. NOTES ON THE *TRACTATUS* AND ITS TRANSLATIONS

There are two translations available of the *Tractatus*. The first of these was undertaken by C.K. Ogden, published by Routledge and Kegan Paul in 1922. But although Ogden was the official translator, a major part of the translation was actually the work of Frank Ramsey, and Wittgenstein himself made extensive comments on the translation as it progressed. Some of the translations, particularly at some of the places where the translation is very free, such as at 4.023, are derived from Wittgenstein's own suggestions. (See Wittgenstein, *Letters to C. K. Ogden* for details.) This translation is certainly not flawless, and dissatisfaction with some aspects of it led D.F. Pears and B.F. McGuinness to produce a second version, published in 1961, also by Routledge and Kegan Paul.

Both translations are serviceable, and to a large extent it is a matter of personal preference which translation one uses. Despite the fact that it contains some mistakes that have been corrected in the later version, I myself prefer the Ogden version as better capturing the spirit of the original, and as containing a number of particularly happy renderings. The following specific points about the two translations should be borne in mind:

- Although the Ogden translation has the authority derived from the fact that Wittgenstein made extensive comments on it, and even contributed to it, it should be remembered that although Wittgenstein was fluent in English, he was not a native speaker, and had only been resident in England for a relatively short time, so that his appreciation of the nuances of English will not have been perfect, so that even if Wittgenstein's approval of a certain translation is to be taken seriously, he is not to be regarded as necessarily infallible.

• The translation of one pair of terms in particular should be noted. Ogden translates '*Sachverhalt*' and '*Sachlage*' as 'atomic fact' and 'state of affairs' respectively. Of these, 'atomic fact' is derived from Russellian terminology, but is potentially misleading, since although one cannot speak of a non-existent fact, a Wittgensteinian *Sachverhalt* may or may not exist. Wittgenstein himself disliked 'state of affairs', but could not suggest any better. Pears and McGuinness by contrast translate '*Sachverhalt*' and '*Sachlage*' as 'state of affairs' and 'situation'. There is obviously a potential source of confusion here, and the only thing that the reader can do about it is to be aware of this divergence when reading the different translations or commentaries on them. In this book I have, in common with most commentators, followed Pears and McGuinness here.

• There is one particular respect in which the Ogden translation is definitely at fault. There are certain words that Wittgenstein uses as semi-technical terms throughout the *Tractatus*. In these cases, what matters is not so much which English words are adopted for their translation, as that the translation should be consistent. There are two pairs of terms where this is especially important – '*darstellen*' and '*abbilden*', and '*sinnlos*' and '*unsinnig*'. In each case, Wittgenstein clearly differentiates these concepts. See here 2.201 and 4.461–4.4611. Although Ogden uses the pairs of terms 'depict' and 'represent' and 'without sense' and 'nonsense' in these key passages, he does not adhere consistently to these translations, and will frequently translate '*abbilden*' by 'represent' and both '*sinnlos*' and '*unsinnig*' by 'senseless', with potentially highly misleading results: thus at 6.54 has Wittgenstein claimed that the sentences of his book are 'senseless', which in the terminology of the *Tractatus* would imply that they were vacuous truths of logic, whereas the whole point of the book is the much stronger claim that they are simply nonsense. Therefore the reader of the *Tractatus* who is working with the Ogden translation should develop the habit of checking what word is used in the German whenever these words occur in the English.

In this book itself I have not slavishly followed one or other of the two standard translations, but either chosen whichever of the two seems to capture the original best, or given my own rendering.

2. BIOGRAPHICAL

B.F. McGuiness, *Wittgenstein, a Life.*
A thoroughly researched and readable biography of Wittgenstein up to 1921.

3. OTHER RELEVANT TEXTS BY WITTGENSTEIN

Notebooks 1914–16
This book has the most direct relevance to the *Tractatus* of all. I discuss the use that should be made of the *Notebooks* at the beginning of Chapter 3.

'Some Remarks on Logical Form'.
Philosophical Remarks.
Philosophical Grammar.
Philosophical Investigations.

For comments on these later works by Wittgenstein, see the 'Reception and Influence' section of this book.

4. SOME RELEVANT WORKS BY FREGE, RUSSELL AND RAMSEY

Frege, *The Foundations of Arithmetic.*
From a purely philosophical point of view this is Frege's masterpiece. It is revolutionary in its philosophical implications, and yet is written with beautiful clarity, and is strongly recommended, even apart from its relevance for Wittgenstein's work. However, there is much less evidence in the *Tractatus* itself of its influence on Wittgenstein's thinking than is the case with *The Basic Laws of Arithmetic.* The major exception to this is the so-called 'Context Principle' – 'a word has meaning only in the context of a sentence' (cf. *Tractatus* 3.3 and 3.314). Wittgenstein recurs to *this* idea throughout his philosophical writings, both early and late.

The Basic Laws of Arithmetic.

This is the work in which Frege attempted the full implementation of the 'logicist' programme – the presentation of the truths of number theory as theorems derivable from a small set of basic logical axioms. The big flaw in the system was that it includes an axiom (Vb) that makes it possible to derive a contradiction within the system. Internal evidence indicates that at the time of writing the *Tractatus* this was the text of Frege's that Wittgenstein' had most studied, and in particular the introductory prose sections of Volume I.

Russell, *Principles of Mathematics.*

This book may well have been among the influences that led Wittgenstein first to become interested in the foundations of mathematics, and hence philosophy.

'The Philosophy of Logical Atomism'.

It is worthwhile comparing and contrasting Russell's version of logical atomism with the *Tractatus.*

F. P. Ramsey: 'The Foundations of Mathematics'.

The opening pages of this article still remain one of the best introductions to the logical doctrines of the *Tractatus.*

5. SOME MORE RECENT BOOKS ON THE *TRACTATUS*

Anthony Kenny, *Wittgenstein.*

I place this book first as containing a remarkably clear introduction to the *Tractatus.* Although I disagree with a number of his interpretations, it is also far more reliable than most of what has been written on the *Tractatus.*

G.E.M. Anscombe, *An Introduction to Wittgenstein's Tractatus.*

Despite its title, undergraduates tend to find this book difficult. It is, however, one of the philosophically most penetrating studies.

Erik Stenius, *Wittgenstein's Tractatus.*

Although disappointing on the logical aspects of the book, this is in other respects well worth reading. Particularly interesting (whether he is right or wrong) is his comparison of Wittgenstein and Kant.

James Griffin, *Wittgenstein's Logical Atomism*.

As its title indicates, an interesting exploration of the 'atomism' of the *Tractatus*, although I think he is completely wrong as to what the objects of the *Tractatus* might be.

A. Crary and R. Read (eds.), *The New Wittgenstein*.

For those interested in learning further about the 'New Wittgenstein' (see Section 7, '4. A "Therapeutic" Reading'), this is a representative selection of articles.

6. SOME ARTICLES ON THE *TRACTATUS*

P.T. Geach, 'Wittgenstein's Operator N'.
R.M. White, 'Wittgenstein on Identity'.

These two articles are helpful on some of the strictly logical aspects of the *Tractatus*.

P.T. Geach, 'Saying and Showing in Wittgenstein and Frege'.

A key article on the saying/showing distinction.
P.M. Simons, 'The Old Problem of Complex and Fact'.

An excellent study of Wittgenstein's conception of analysis.
P.M. Sullivan, 'The Totality of Facts', 'A Version of the Picture Theory', 'Wittgenstein's Context Principle'.

Many of the best recent articles on the *Tractatus* have been those of Peter Sullivan. These three in particular are well worth reading.

NOTES

1: CONTEXT

1 Letter to Russell, 6 May 1920 (*Notebooks 1914–16* [ed. G.H. von Wright and G.E.M. Anscombe; 2nd edn; Blackwell: Oxford, 1979], p. 132).

2 Susan Sterrett explored these possible influences in *Wittgenstein Flies a Kite* (Pi Press: New York, 2006).

2: OVERVIEW OF THEMES

1 L. Wittgenstein, *Tractatus Logico-Philosophicus* (trans. C.K. Ogden; Routledge: London, 1922; trans. D.F. Pears and B.F. McGuinness; Routledge: London, 1961), Author's Preface, p. 3.

2 L. Wittgenstein, *Philosophical Remarks* (ed. R. Rhees; trans. R. Hargreaves and R.M. White; Blackwell: Oxford, 1975), p. 55.

3 Wittgenstein, *Notebooks*, p. 79.

3: READING THE *TRACTATUS*

1 D. Lee, *Wittgenstein's Lectures, Cambridge 1930–32* (Blackwell: Oxford, 1980), p. 119.

2 As an introduction to the modern philosophical discussion, the right starting point is the debate between P.F. Strawson and J.L. Austin. See Strawson, 'Truth', in *PAS* Supp. vol. 24 (1950): 129–56 and Austin, 'Unfair to Facts' (1954, reprinted in J.L. Austin, *Philosophical Papers* [ed. J.O. Urmson and G.J. Warnock; OUP: Oxford, 1970]).

3 See Wittgenstein, *Philosophical Remarks*, Appendix 'Complex and Fact' (pp. 301–303).

4 See, e.g., Wittgenstein, *Notebooks*, p. 48.

5 Ibid.

6 See, e.g., Wittgenstein, *Philosophical Remarks*, pp. 105–14.

7 Lee, *Wittgenstein's Lectures*, p. 119.

8 There is a complication here that needs mentioning though it should not detain us at this stage. At different points in the *Tractatus* Wittgenstein

seems to conceive logical space in two different ways. According to the first conception, which is the one I am sketching here, the points of logical space are occupied by states of affairs, according to the other, by 'possible worlds'. You need the first conception if you want to explain how one builds a complete picture of the *actual* world out of propositions representing discrete states of affairs; you need the second, if you want to give a complete account of the truth-conditions of a proposition. Wittgenstein, as I say, seems to oscillate between these two conceptions. If we were fully to work out the metaphor of logical space, we would need a more complicated structure for that space than would be given by either conception taken separately.

9 NB if you are using the Ogden translation, Ogden translates *Sachverhalt* as 'atomic fact' and *Sachlage* as 'state of affairs'. I am following Pears and McGuinness in translating 'these two terms as 'state of affairs' and 'situation', respectively.

10 Wittgenstein, *Notebooks*, p. 48.

11 Compare Wittgenstein's own later discussion in the appendix to *Philosophical Remarks* entitled 'Complex and Fact'.

12 It goes without saying that this is an artificially simple example used for illustrative purposes only, and that the actual analysis of an object into its constituents would proceed along far more complicated lines than this: and in particular, in the light of what I said earlier, there is no reason to suppose that the constituents of an object such as a teapot would be its physically smaller parts.

13 See Lee, *Wittgenstein's Lectures*, p. 120.

14 Wittgenstein, *Notebooks*, pp. 20–21.

15 At 4.04, Wittgenstein refers to H. Hertz's *Die Prinzipien der Mechanik in neuem Zusammenhange dargestellt* (ed. Philipp Lenard; J.A. Bath: Leipzig, 1894) in this connection, and this suggests that the use of models in physics and engineering may well be one of the significant influences on Wittgenstein that led him to think of propositions as pictures. Hertz proposes that a scientific theory may be regarded as a model of the physical reality that it talks about: the 'Picture Theory' of the *Tractatus* can be viewed as a generalization of that idea to language as a whole.

16 Readers using Ogden's translation should be warned that although this is his main translation, he does not stick to it consistently, and sometimes translates '*Abbildung*' as 'representation' too, which can on occasion mislead, unless you check the German text.

17 Compare on this point, *Philosophical Remarks*, section III.

18 The relevant *Notebook* entries are in particular those from 14 June 1915 to 22 June 1915 on pp. 59–71.

19 Wittgenstein, *Notebooks*, p. 69.

20 Ibid., p. 62.

21 Ibid., p. 64.

22 Ibid., p. 61.

23 Ibid., p. 64.

24 Ibid.

25 It is worth noting that in the *Notebooks* entry from which 3.24 comes, after the sentence: 'That a propositional element signifies a complex can be seen from an indeterminacy in the propositions in which it occurs', Wittgenstein writes: 'This stems from the generality of such propositions'. This addition certainly helps to clarify his meaning, and it seems perverse that in the *Tractatus* he should have omitted this sentence from an already highly compressed passage.

26 See in particular L. Wittgenstein, *Philosophical Investigations* (trans. G.E.M. Anscombe; Blackwell: Oxford, 1953), §§92–97.

27 G. Frege, *The Foundations of Arithmetic*, (1884; trans. J.L. Austin; Blackwell: Oxford, 1959), Introduction, p. x.

28 Wittgenstein, *Notebooks*, p. 97.

29 Ibid., p. 106.

30 If we were to read 'Nothing is F' as 'No thing is F', it would then be equivalent to the absurd 'Anything (or "Any thing") which is F is not a thing'.

31 Cf. his letter to Russell at the end of 1913 (*Notebooks*, p. 129): '. . . your Theory of Descriptions is *quite* UNDOUBTEDLY right, even though the individual primitive signs are quite different from what you think they are.'

32 Wittgenstein, *Philosophical Investigations*, §66.

33 Robert Fogelin objected (*Wittgenstein* [2nd edn.; Routledge: London, 1987], p. 78) that Wittgenstein's use of the N-operator would permit him to explain simple generalizations ['$(x)fx$' or '$(\exists x)fx$'], but Wittgenstein's account of the general form of proposition would not generate propositions of mixed multiple generality ['$(\exists x)(y)f(x, y)$']. Here we need to bear in mind the discussion of Frege that we included in the 'Context' section of this book. It is possible to generate such propositions, but only by a two-stage process. At the first stage, we use the N-operator to generate all of the propositions '$(y)f(a, y)$', '$(y)f(b, y)$', '$(y)f(c, y)$' . . . We then, as a second stage, define a new propositional variable ranging over all *those* propositions, and by applying the N-operator to that variable, we arrive at the proposition '$(\exists x)(y) . f(x, y)$', negating which gives the required result. Fogelin failed, because he tried to generate such propositions by a single-stage process, which is indeed impossible.

34 See e.g. B. Russell, 'The Philosophy of Logical Atomism' (*The Collected Papers of Bertrand Russell*, vol. 8 [ed. John G. Slater; Allen and Unwin: London, 1986], pp. 164–65, 206–207).

35 Wittgenstein, *Notebooks*, p. 131.

36 Ibid., p. 123.

37 See his introduction to the *Tractatus*, p. 16.

38 See e.g. Anthony Kenny, *Wittgenstein* (1973; rev. edn; Blackwell: Oxford, 2006), p. 80.

39 When he wrote the 5.6s, Wittgenstein must have been aware of the remark attributed to Schopenhauer: 'Every man takes the limits of his own field of vision for the limits of the world'.

40 I. Kant, *Critique of Pure Reason* (trans. N. Kemp Smith; Macmillan: London, 1929), B 131.

41 Ibid., B 399–432.

42 Ibid., B xxx.

43 In fact Russell, in his Introduction to the *Tractatus* (p. 14), gives a satisfactory informal exposition of what Wittgenstein should have said, silently correcting the text of proposition 6, while tactfully saying: 'Mr. Wittgenstein's explanation of his symbolism is not quite fully given in the text'.

44 In fact, very few are required: after the fourth repetition, every truth-function will have appeared.

45 B. Russell, *Introduction to Mathematical Philosophy* (Allen and Unwin: London, 1919), p. 205.

46 The cumbersome notation here is explained by the fact that 6.1203–6.122 is a reworking of material contained in a letter to Russell on November 1913 (see Wittgenstein, *Notebooks*, pp. 125–29). That is to say, the ideas here date from a time before the far simpler and more elegant truth-table notation given elsewhere in the *Tractatus*.

47 Kant, *Critique of Pure Reason*, B208 ff.

48 Wittgenstein, *Notebooks*, pp. 76–91.

49 Ibid., p. 80.

50 In various conversations, Wittgenstein talked of poets as showing what could not be said. That use of the notion of showing seems a far cry from the earlier *logical* doctrines that led him to draw the showing/saying distinction in the first place.

51 Russell, Introduction to the *Tractatus*, p. 22.

52 Wittgenstein, *Tractatus*, Preface, p. 29.

53 This should be taken together with the emphatic remark at 5.61: 'What we cannot think, we cannot think; so what we cannot think we cannot *say* either'.

54 Principally, Cora Diamond and James Conant (see, e.g., A. Crary and R. Read [eds.], *The New Wittgenstein* [Routledge: London, 2000]).

55 Russell's Introduction, p. 23.

56 Wittgenstein, *Notebooks*, p. 132.

57 For a representative set of articles, see Crary and Read, *The New Wittgenstein*.

58 Wittgenstein, *Notebooks*, p. 131.

59 L. Wittgenstein, 'Some Remarks on Logical Form', *PAS* Supp. vol. 9 (1929): 162–71.

60 Charles Dickens, *Great Expectations*, chapter XXIV.

61 G. Frege, *Posthumous Writings* (ed. Hermes, Kambartel and Kaulbach; trans. Long and White; Blackwell: Oxford, 1979), p. 252.

62 Wittgenstein, *Notebooks*, p. 131.

63 Note, however, that in 5.62 Wittgenstein is prepared to talk of 'a truth' (*eine Wahrheit*).

4: RECEPTION AND INFLUENCE

1 See in particular, Wittgenstein, *Philosophical Remarks*, section IX.

2 Ibid., p. 115.

3 Ibid., p. 51.

4 A 'phenomenological language' would be one in which propositions were analysed into propositions describing immediate experience.

5 Wittgenstein, *Philosophical Investigations*, p. x.

6 In §§23, 46, 97 and 114. One should also include §65, where although the *Tractatus* is not mentioned the reference to his earlier book is clear.

7 One point to note is that in §48 he completely ignores the insistence in the *Tractatus* that a propositional sign was a fact and not a complex object (3.14), and all his criticisms are directed against the propositional sign considered as a complex object.

BIBLIOGRAPHY

Anscombe, G.E.M., *An Introduction to Wittgenstein's Tractatus* (Hutchinson: London, 1959).

Austin, J.L., 'Unfair to Facts' (1954; reprinted in Austin, *Philosophical Papers*, 154–74).

— *Philosophical Papers* (ed. J.O. Urmson and G.J. Warnock; OUP: Oxford, 1970).

Crary, A. and Read, R. (eds.), *The New Wittgenstein* (Routledge: London, 2000).

Fogelin, R.J., *Wittgenstein* (2nd edn; Routledge: London, 1987).

Frege, G., *Begriffsschrift* (Verlag von Louis Nebert: Halle, 1879 [trans. *Conceptual Notation* by T. W. Bynum; OUP: Oxford, 1972]).

— 'On Sense and Reference' (1892) in *Translations from the Philosophical Writings of Gottlob Frege* (ed. and trans. P.T. Geach and M. Black, Blackwell: Oxford, 1952), 56–78.

— *Foundations of Arithmetic* (1884; trans. J.L. Austin; Blackwell: Oxford, 1959).

— *The Basic Laws of Arithmetic* (Vol. I, 1893; trans. and ed. Montgomery Furth; University of California: Berkeley, 1964).

— *Posthumous Writings* (ed. Hermes, Kambartel and Kaulbach; trans. Long and White; Blackwell: Oxford, 1979).

Geach, P.T., 'Wittgenstein's Operator N', *Analysis* 41 (1981): 168–70.

— 'Saying and Showing in Wittgenstein and Frege', in Hintikka, *Essays in Honor of G.H. von Wright*.

Griffin, James, *Wittgenstein's Logical Atomism* (OUP: Oxford, 1964).

Hertz, H. (ed. Philipp Lenard), *Die Prinzipien der Mechanik in neuem Zusammenhange dargestellt* (J.A. Barth: Leipzig, 1894).

Hintikka, J. (ed.), *Essays in Honor of G. H. von Wright, Acta Philosophica Fennica* 28 (North-Holland Pub. Co: Amsterdam, 1976).

Kant, I. *Critique of Pure Reason* (1781, 1787; trans. N. Kemp Smith; Macmillan: London, 1929).

Kenny, Anthony, *Wittgenstein* (1973; rev. edn; Blackwell: Oxford, 2006).

Lee, D. (ed.), *Wittgenstein's Lectures, Cambridge 1930–32* (Blackwell: Oxford, 1980).

McGuinness, B.F., *Wittgenstein, a Life: Young Ludwig (1889–1921)* (Duckworth: London, 1988).

Ramsey, F.P., 'The Foundations of Mathematics' (1925; reprinted in Ramsey, *Philosophical Papers*, 164–224).

— *Philosophical Papers* (ed. D.H. Mellor; CUP: Cambridge, 1990).

Russell, Bertrand, *Principles of Mathematics* (Allen and Unwin: London, 1903).

— 'The Philosophy of Logical Atomism' (1918, reprinted in Russell, *Collected Papers 8*).

— *Introduction to Mathematical Philosophy* (Allen and Unwin: London, 1919).

— Introduction to Wittgenstein's *Tractatus*.

— *Collected Papers 8: The Philosophy of Logical Atomism and Other Essays* (1914–19; ed. John G. Slater; Allen and Unwin: London, 1986).

Simons, P.M., 'The Old Problem of Complex and Fact' (1983; reprinted in Simons, *Philosophy and Logic*, 319–38).

— *Philosophy and Logic in Central Europe from Bolzano to Tarski* (Kluwer: Dordrecht, 1992).

Stenius, Erik, *Wittgenstein's Tractatus* (Blackwell: Oxford, 1975).

Sterrett, Susan, *Wittgenstein Flies a Kite* (Pi Press: New York, 2006).

Strawson, P.F. 'Truth', in *PAS* Supp. vol. 24 (1950): 129–56.

Sullivan, P.M., 'The Totality of Facts', in *PAS* 100 (2000): 175–92.

— 'A Version of the Picture Theory', in W. Vossenkuhl, 2001: *Wittgenstein*, 2001, 89–110.

— 'Wittgenstein's Context Principle', in W. Vossenkuhl, *Wittgenstein*, 65–88.

Vossenkuhl, W. (ed.), *Wittgenstein: Tractatus – Klassiker Auslegen* (Akademie Verlag: Berlin, 2001).

White, R.M., 'Wittgenstein on Identity', *PAS* 78 (1978): 157–74.

Whitehead, A.N. and Russell, B., *Principia Mathematica*, vol. I (CUP: Cambridge, 1st edn 1910, 2nd edn 1925).

Wittgenstein, L., *Notebooks 1914–16* (ed. G.H. von Wright and G.E.M. Anscombe; 2nd edn; Blackwell: Oxford, 1979).

— *Letters to C. K. Ogden* (Blackwell: Oxford, 1973).

— *Tractatus Logico-Philosophicus* (trans. C.K. Ogden; Routledge: London, 1922; trans. D.F. Pears and B.F. McGuinness; Routledge: London, 1961).

— 'Some Remarks on Logical Form', *PAS* Supp. vol. 9 (1929): 162–71.

— *Philosophical Remarks* (ed. R. Rhees; trans. R. Hargreaves and R.M. White; Blackwell: Oxford, 1975).

— *Philosophical Grammar* (ed. R. Rhees; trans. A. Kenny; Blackwell: Oxford, 1974).

— *The Big Typescript TS 213* (ed. and trans. C.G. Luckhardt and M.A.E. Aue; Blackwell: Oxford, 2005).

— *Philosophical Investigations* (trans. G.E.M. Anscombe; Blackwell: Oxford, 1953).

INDEX

abbilden/Abbildung ('depict'/
   'depiction') 145, 150
   see also depiction; pictures;
   representation
absolute generality 24, 117
agenda for philosophy set by
   Tractatus 137
analysis
   of the language of science 139
   and objects 36–7, 41–2, 150
   of propositions 54, 57–9, 102
analytic philosophy 135–6, 139
Anscombe, G.E.M. 20, 147, 149,
   151
Aristotle 3–4
arithmetic *see* number theory
atomic fact 145, 150
atomic propositions 79, 95
atomistic conception of language
   139
Austin, J.L. 149
axioms 4–5, 6, 7, 8, 107–8

being/non-being of elements 37
beliefs expressed in propositions
   98
bestimmt/Bestimmtheit
   ('determinate'/
   'determinacy') 55
   see also determinacy of sense;
   specificity; vagueness
Boltzmann, Ludwig 2–3
Brahms, Johannes 1

Carnap, Rudolf 135, 136, 138
causal laws 112, 137
Church, Alonzo 106–7, 108
'colour exclusion problem' 34, 139,
   140
combinations
   of expressions 64
   of objects 36, 37
   of signs 94
complex objects 36–7, 151
   facts as 31–3
   names of 32–3, 42, 54, 57–60
   and simple objects 36–7
complex propositions 72, 73
   constructed of simple
   propositions 78–9
complex, theory of the 31–2, 40–2,
   44, 54, 151
compositional language 71–2, 82,
   136
Conant, James 152
concepts, formal and genuine 77–8,
   116
conditions for the possibility of
   language 44, 93, 115–16, 124
connectives 84
constituents
   of complexes 40–2
   of pictures 43–4
Context Principle 5, 30, 62–5, 136,
   146
contingent entities/propositions 41,
   104